WESTMAR COLLE

Hustlers,
Beats,
and Others

OBSERVATIONS

A series edited by Howard S. Becker
Northwestern University

Hustlers, Beats, and Others

by NED POLSKY

ALDINE Publishing Company/*Chicago*

First published 1967 by
Aldine Publishing Company
320 West Adams Street
Chicago, Illinois 60606

Library of Congress Catalog Card Number 67-11416
Designed by Bernard Schleifer
Printed in the United States of America

For Arline

Preface

This book is about the sociology of deviance. The differences among the chapters are in basic approach to the subject as well as in substantive content: one chapter reports on field research that relied heavily on participant observation, and another reports on field research that did not; a third chapter is a study in historical sociology; a fourth analyzes questions of research method; and the fifth is an exercise in theory.

The chapters cohere not only because of their concern with the sociology of deviance, but because all of them sharply disagree with the accepted views (sociological or otherwise) of their respective subjects. I have excluded those writings of mine on deviance that seem, on hindsight, to have differed merely in detail from the work of predecessors. Albrecht Dürer's insistence that the chief task of the artist was to "pour out new things which had never before been in the mind of any other man" has always struck me as the only decent attitude to take toward one's intellectual endeavors. Whether the "new things" in this book are also true or beautiful is for the reader to decide; but at least he will find much that is new, will find that every chapter radically dissents from one or more received opinions.

In another respect I have tried to give the reader more for his money than is usual. That is the result of special circumstance which it may be edifying to relate.

Back when I was publishing scholarly books instead of writing one, I would frequently reject a manuscript by sending the author a letter like the following: "You have things to say that are both new and useful. But all that is new and conceivably useful can easily be said in a 20-page article. I don't see much point in distending it to 300-odd pages." (Actually, I had to hold tight rein on such letters, for had I followed all my inclinations to send them I would have been left with hardly any books to publish.) The realization grew that these manuscripts resulted not merely from the moronic promotion standards of American universities—according to which one book is held automatically to be "worth" several articles—but equally from the scholar's natural addiction to vacuities. I resolved that whatever the defects of any book by myself, it would not have *that* defect, but would be as tightly packed as possible.

The desire to present much material in little space makes for a pinched utilitarian style, laden with footnotes, lacking in simile and metaphor, heavily adjectival, flat-footedly direct, and difficult for readers inclined to skim. I note the fact for literary gents and pass on to consider other aspects of style that might be more annoying to the scholar.

The book's vocabulary comes from several different bags. I don't believe in the alleged natural superiority of a diction that takes care always to stick to one "level of usage" and to preserve "unity of tone." I use whatever words that I think will most neatly convey my exact meaning, whether polysyllabic technical words or lowbrow slang words, fashionable words or unfashionable words, serious words or funny words. It bothers me not a bit that words having very different social statuses cohabit in my prose. A few readers agree, and even find such democracy exhilarating; most readers find it merely jarring.

Many readers of this book will feel that I object to the views of other scholars in terms that are overly fierce. These days the more usual mode in academia, thronged as it is with *arrivistes* aspiring to be gentlemen, is to voice such objections oleaginously. But luckily I cut an eyetooth on that masterpiece of English prose, A. E. Housman's introduction to his edition of

Manilius, and so am forever immune to the notion that polemical writing and scholarly writing shouldn't mix. I believe that polemical scholarship improves the quality of intellectual life—sharpens the mind, helps get issues settled faster—by forcing genteel discussion to become genuine debate.

Although we learn from many teachers, there is a very special debt owed to the first great teacher whose acquaintance we make, the man who truly opens our eyes. That debt I owe to the late Miles Hanley of the University of Wisconsin—phonetician, historian of the English language, and Chaucerian —who in his practice and precept first showed me the meaning of the life of learning, showed me what genuine scholarship was supposed to be and how to distinguish the real variety from the fake.

Hans Gerth, also of the University of Wisconsin, overcame my humanistic bias that sociology was not worth a serious man's time. From previous contacts with its practitioners, I had concluded that sociology consisted alternately in producing detailed proof of what everyone knew already (platitudes) and producing new knowledge not worth knowing (trivia). Hans Gerth's brilliant lectures convinced me in myriad ways that although this is usually the case, it is not always so—convinced me so fully that I entered the graduate department of sociology at the University of Chicago.

At Chicago I learned much from Herbert Blumer and the late Louis Wirth, among others. My deepest Chicago debt is to a man who gave me the most misery in graduate school, Everett Hughes. I took his course in methods of field research only because it was required, hated it, suffered through it, and did not begin to see its enormous value or apply its lessons until years later. How much my appreciation has grown for Everett Hughes and his work will, I trust, be clear in many of the following pages.

Some material in this book previously appeared in different form in the following periodicals, to which grateful acknowledgment is made: *Dissent, Social Problems,* and *Soundings.*

For providing bibliographical help, I am indebted to Linda Asher, William Cole, Seymour Hacker, James Williams Hoffman, the late Dr. Julian A. Miller, Charles Westoff, Robert Wheeler, Elias Wilentz, and the staffs of the New York Public Library and the New York Historical Society Library.

My research in England connected with chapters 1 and 2 was greatly aided by the British Museum staff, who assiduously located early books on billiards amidst their tangle of sporting books badly hit by World War II bombings. I am indebted more heavily still to John Harris, Keeper of the Drawings Collection at the Royal Institute of British Architects, for instructing me in procedures of research on English architectural history, for making available to me his personal library of rare early guidebooks to country houses, and for many other kindnesses.

An early draft of chapter 1 was read critically by Robert B. Silvers; Erving Goffman criticized a draft of chapter 2 and, along with John F. Gallagher, gave me similar help on chapter 4. I have gained much from their advice. Howard Becker instigated this book, nagged me until it was done, read the entire manuscript, and made many improvements in it.

Feeling my lack of adequate words to indicate just how great a debt is owed my wife, to whom this book is dedicated, I consulted prefaces of other books, intending to pick out the most apt phrase and use it here. I found the choice to be hopeless, for every one of the many sweet things authors write about their wives is true of mine.

NED POLSKY

Contents

Hustlers,
Beats,
and Others

1
Of Pool Playing and Poolrooms

A Study in Historical Sociology*

The game of pool, or "pocket billiards" as the men who make playing equipment or run the fancier poolrooms would like you to call it, has been undergoing a renaissance. This revival, accidentally touched off by the enormous success of the movie *The Hustler* (late 1961, re-released 1964), has been kept going via an adroit and energetic public relations campaign by certain sporting equipment manufacturers, chiefly Brunswick. The manufacturers are running scared: bowling alleys have been overbuilt, and equipment makers are faced not only with declining demand but the prospect of having to repossess thousands of automatic pinsetters, costing $9,000 each, which they have financed on long-term notes. Thus the attempt to cash in on *The Hustler* and revive pool and billiards. The campaign just might work, for such a reversal of fashion is not without precedent in our sports history; an observer wrote in 1869 that "Popular favor for ten-pins having about this time—the close of 1858—yielded to the superior attraction of billiards, Mr. Kingsley changed his alleys into a poolroom devoted to the latter game." [1]

The current upsurge in pool playing is not nearly as impressive as many press releases and planted feature stories

---

* Part of this essay was presented at the annual meeting of the Eastern Sociological Society, New York City, April, 1965, and appeared in *Soundings* (State University of New York, Stony Brook), Vol. 2, No. 1, Spring, 1965.

[1] Cf. Dudley Kavanagh, *The Billiard World* (New York: Kavanagh & Decker, 1869), p. 27.

would have one believe. Four decades ago the number of
American poolrooms was four times what it is today, and on a
per capita basis (number of pool and billiard tables compared
with the total population) poolrooms were then about ten
times as popular as they are now after three years of "revival."
But there has undoubtedly been a recent growth of interest in
poolroom games, after more than three decades of unrelieved
decline: witness the installing of many pool and billiard tables
in bowling establishments; a sharp rise in the sale of private
tables to suburban homeowners; pool contests on nationwide
television; and most importantly, the opening of more than
3,000 new poolrooms.[2]

As one whose chief recreation since the age of 13 has been
billiards, I am as much in favor of renewed public interest in
poolrooms as any professional yea-sayer in the industry. But
sociological analysis of the available historical data, reported
below, forces me to conclude that the present revival will soon
peter out, and that American per capita participation in poolroom games will never again become even a sixth of what it
once was.

In this conclusion I am in sorrowful disagreement with the
manufacturers and poolroom owners, who at this improved
moment in their fortunes are understandably optimists almost to
a man. Recollecting, as they do, the once-great popularity of
poolrooms, they believe that the revival will not only be maintained but hugely expanded. Moreover, they are confident that
they have hit upon a method to assure this end.

Being aware of the moral stigma attached to poolrooms,
they place faith in publicly and loudly casting out sin—the
method of "deviance disavowal" as the sociologist has it, or of
"upgrading" one's "image" as the adman has it. In the poolroom business this process is known as "cleaning up the game,"
and currently it revolves about such things as installing carpets
and bright lights and pastel colors, curbing obscene language,
getting rid of hustlers and hoodlums and alcoholics, and try-

[2] For statistics on the number of poolrooms and pool and billiard
tables, see note 42.

ing to bring women in. On the advice of public relations coun-
sel, the trade has also given outward and visible sign of the inward and spiritual grace by undergoing rebaptism: "poolrooms"
have been replaced by "billiard lounges."

Lately the trade has, in addition, made use of public relations men in the latter's role as inventors and purveyors of
conscious, deliberate falsehoods.[3] To give but one example:
The 1963 world professional pocket billiard (pool) tournament saw the emergence of a new champion, Luther Lassiter,
who later won the 1964 tournament as well. Now the central
fact of Lassiter's previous occupational life is that he had been
for many years, under the monicker of "Wimpy," a genuine
pool hustler of the old school—indeed such a good one that
many of his hustler colleagues had long acknowledged his su-
premacy in one form of the grift, the game of nine ball.[4] But
the public relations men who now write of Lassiter alternately
suppress and blatantly deny this, and their fabrications are con-
veyed to mass audiences by reporters who conceive of journal-
ism as the rephrasing of press handouts (see, for example, the
mindless article on pool in the *Saturday Evening Post* of April
18, 1964).

In this access of real and imagined virtue the manufacturers and poolroom owners are proceeding, I think, on a mistaken assumption. They subscribe to the commonly accepted
view that the game's popularity waned because of the growing
association of poolrooms, in the public mind, with gamblers,
loafers, criminals and the like. It seems to me that the historical
evidence reveals this explanation to be dead wrong, and that
poolrooms instead declined because of certain long-term
changes in America's social structure that are, apparently,
irreversible.

[3] This sort of thing poses ticklish research problems in any study
that must, like this one, draw upon mass periodicals for some source
material. Over four-fifths of the news items in the modern newspaper,
and the large majority of articles in most mass magazines, derive from
material supplied by public relations men, publicity men, official press
representatives and the like—men whose jobs require them to serve with
extraordinary frequency as professional liars.

[4] The following chapter explores what the hustler is and does.

I

The historical evidence on pool or any other sport is not conveniently "given" and merely awaiting sociological analysis. In this regard the sociologist, concerned with tracing how the history of an American sport is related to such things as social structure and social change, finds himself confronted with two unanticipated research problems.

His first special problem is that America's professional historians have not done what might be deemed their part of the job. Some of their works on various historical periods give, to be sure, once-over-lightly accounts of sports and games popular at different times; and they have written surveys of American sports history as such, the most notable being John Krout's *Annals of American Sport* (1929) and Foster Rhea Dulles' *America Learns to Play* (1940). But except possibly for baseball, the grand total of professional historical writing on any particular American sport does not begin to resemble a reasonably detailed and reliable history of that sport—whether social history or any other kind.

A related problem is that amateurs have rushed in where professionals fear to tread, and have set many traps for the unwary researcher. Much published material that calls itself the history of this or that sport is, in considerable part, nonsense. It may be found in the introductory sections or appendices of instruction manuals on sports, in encyclopedia articles, and in specialized periodicals about sports. The writer of such "history" sometimes is professionally connected with the sport, sometimes is a devoted fan, but in any case is not trained to do historical research. Some of his material is unavoidably important and must be drawn upon, especially if it gives an eyewitness account behind which one can detect no ulterior motive or sloppiness or undue play of the writer's imagination. But even when written out of purest intent, almost invariably this material contains much that is demonstrably wrong.

Quite representative of the genre are the historical discussions in the two latest billiard instruction books.[5] Their accounts of events beyond living memory are uncritically compiled from secondary sources and repeat errors that infest even the best of these sources (such as the *Encyclopaedia Britannica* and Frank Menke's *New Encyclopedia of Sports*).[They tell us, for example, that billiards entered America about 1565 when Spaniards brought a form of the game to St. Augustine; but my own research on the American history of billiards has failed to uncover any reference before the late seventeenth century. The notion that the American game began over a century earlier is a myth passed on from one lazy billiard historian to the next; hardly one of them has ever bothered his head about finding a primary source for the alleged fact of sixteenth-century origin, which isn't surprising when you consider that most such "historians" don't know there is such a thing as a distinction between primary and secondary sources.[6]]

The real pity in the lunkhead tradition of cobbling together secondary material is that just a little original searching reveals all sorts of useful data never cited by any sports historian, amateur or professional. Let us look at some of these data.

II

As soon as one begins seriously to examine primary sources, the standard explanation for the decline of poolrooms collapses. Material from every historical period reveals one fact overwhelmingly: poolrooms *always* had "middle-class morality" very solidly against them, were *always* highly stigmatized. This opposition to public poolrooms even extended, on occasion, to

[5] Cf. the historical sections in Luther Lassiter, *The Modern Guide to Pocket Billiards* (New York: Fleet Publishing Co., 1964), and in Clive Cottingham, Jr., *The Game of Billiards* (Philadelphia: Lippincott & Co., 1965).

[6] An honorable exception, who is not faultless but sees some of the myths for what they are, is the anonymous author of *Modern Billiards* (New York: Brunswick-Balke-Collender Co., 1908), pp. 5–6. His warnings have gone unheeded by later writers on billiard history except Louise Belden, *op. cit. infra,* note 31.

private playing at home by the ultrarespectable.⌐When President
John Quincy Adams installed a billiard table in the White
House (with his own money), his opponents in Congress were
able to raise a big stink about this acquiring of "gambling
furniture" and to use the purchase as campaign material against
him in the election of 1828.⁷⌐

Literally hundreds of sources show that from the very beginning in America of public poolrooms (which started out as
adjuncts to taverns and roadside inns), and uninterruptedly
throughout their history, they were always associated with gambling and various forms of low life, ministers were always de-
nouncing them, police were always finding wanted criminals in
them, and parents were always warning their children to stay
out of them. Here, for example, is Jerome Keogh, world's pool
champion five times between 1897 and 1910, reminiscing about
the 1890's:

> Despite the vaunted glamour of the great billiard acad-
> emies of the gay nineties . . . the fact was that during this
> period "nice" young men stole surreptitiously through
> the by-ways of the night to enter them, lest detection
> should result in the stigma of being "fast." . . . The
> game struggled against the dictates of society, the raising
> of eyebrows, and the word "pool" uttered with caustic
> venom. ⁸

Moreover, poolrooms grew steadily in popularity despite
the fact that, at times, opposition to them was far more severe
than that encountered during the era of their decline. In some
parts of the country there were periods when they could not
even advertise their existence but had to remain hidden from
passing view and draw their customers strictly by word of
mouth. When the playwright William Dunlap of New York visited Baltimore in 1806, for example, he wrote home as follows:

> I have seen several counting houses open on sunday with
> the clarks at work; & Billiard tables publicky notefied

---

⁷ Cf. Samuel Flagg Bemis, *John Quincy Adams and the Union*
(New York: Alfred A. Knopf, 1956), p. 94.

⁸ Quoted in Russell J. Phillips, "Jerome Keogh Opens Palatial
Room in Rochester, New York," *Billiards Magazine* (Chicago), June,
1932, pp. 14–15.

by sign boards. From the first I onely infer that less attention is paid to appearances here than to the northward; & from the second that gambling is not in such *general* disrepute.[9]

III

⌊ It is true that England exported billiards to America with no stigma attached to it. Billiards entered America as "the gentleman's game." But at home in England, the social context of billiard playing had long been more complex than that oftquoted phrase reveals. It is instructive to look at this complexity, because it foreshadowed similar developments that began in America soon after billiards arrived.

Much of early English billiard history is obscure, and much of what Englishmen have written about it is absurd—one unfortunate parallel with America being that English professional historians have also left the subject to incompetent amateurs.[10] But the main point of that history for our purposes is clear enough: billiard playing in England involved two separate, equally important traditions.⌉

[9] *Diary of William Dunlap* (New York: New York Historical Society, 1930), Vol. 2, p. 376.

[10] No English billiard historian has even compiled a halfway reliable bibliography of his subject. Some (by no means all) of the most serious bibliographical problems are as follows:

(1) The best-known early British book on billiards, E. White's *The Game of Billiards* (London: W. Miller, 1807), seems on internal evidence to be largely an unacknowledged translation of a French manual, but no one has tried to confirm this or even taken account of the internal evidence. (2) English billiard historians unanimously, and American counterparts with one exception, agree that White's is the first English-language book on billiards (see, for example, the *Encyclopaedia Britannica*). They are wrong. (3) The exception is Louise Belden, *op. cit. infra*, note 31, who cites a book by John Dew as "*Treatise on the Game of Billiards* (London, 1799)." But as a separately issued publication, Dew's treatise seems to be a ghost. I cannot find it in the catalogues of the British Museum, Ashley Library, London Library, Patent Office (London), Edinburgh University Library, Library of Congress, and Bibliothèque Nationale, or in the National Union Catalogue, or in Robert Watt's *Bibliotheca Britannica,* or in the lists of new books in the *Gentleman's Magazine* for 1799 and the *Annual Register* for 1799. (4) But there is another book earlier than White's, cited by

The first in point of time, and the one exported to America, comprised "respectable" playing by the upper class, which flourished especially in country houses.¹¹ It is difficult to determine the dates of country-house billiard rooms because such rooms were often additions, i.e., were converted from rooms initially devoted to other uses, and because the original architectural plans (unlike the ground plans published much later in

---

no one, in the British Museum. It is an anonymous work ("By an Amateur") of 72 duodecimo pages entitled *Game of Billiards* (London: T. Hurst, 1801). And in it, p. [10], is a reference to playing instructions "laid down by Mr. Dew." (5) A still earlier English book on billiards was almost certainly published in 1772; the "Catalogue of New Publications" in the *Gentleman's Magazine* for that year (Vol. 42, p. 140) has this entry:

The Odds of the Game of Billiards; accurately calculated by a Gentleman who has studied them many Years. To which are added some observations on the Game, that should be attended by every Player. 12mo. 1s. Bladon.

The book is also listed in *Bibliotheca Britannica*. Apparently no copy of this 1772 volume survives.

The bibliography of British writing on billiards to be found elsewhere than in billiard books (e.g., periodicals, diaries, general books on sports and games) is in still worse shape—but I have no space to deal with this.

¹¹ Among early guidebooks to country houses that mention billiard rooms are the following: Anon., *Aedes Pembrochianae: Being a New and Critical Account . . . of the Antiquities at Wilton-House* (London: R. Baldwin, 1744), p. 45; J. Seely, *Stowe: A Description of the House and Gardens* (Buckingham: The Author, 1797), pp. 43, 49 (Stowe had two billiard rooms; its two regular billiard tables are listed in the sale catalogue of 1848, and another, miniature, billiard table is listed in the sale catalogue of 1921); Anon., *A History and Description . . . of Burghley House* (Shrewsbury: J. and W. Eddowes, 1797), p. 126; D. Jacques, *A Visit to Goodwood* (Chichester: The Author, 1822), pp. 48, 52 (Goodwood had two billiard rooms); Anon., *A Description of Hagley, Envil, and the Leasowes* (Birmingham: The Author, n.d. [*ca.* 1765]), p. 136; John Britton, *Graphic Illustrations of Toddington* (London: The Author, 1840), plates [1] and [16] (the latter plate illustrates Toddington's billiard room); John Young, *Catalogue of the Pictures at Leigh Court, Near Bristol* (London: The Proprietor, 1822), p. 27; John Brady, *The Visitor's Guide to Knole* . . . (Sevenoaks: James Payne, 1839), p. 125; William Dean, *An Historical and Descriptive Account of Croome D'Abitot* (Worcester: T. Eaton, 1824), p. 50 (description of the billiard room); Anon., *An Historical and Descriptive Account of Stoke Park in Buckinghamshire* (London: W. Bulmer, 1813), p. [79].

guidebooks) almost never label the use for each room.[12] But there were some billiard rooms of this sort in the last quarter of the sixteenth century. The inventory of Howard House made in 1588 lists "a billyard bord covered wth a green cloth wth a frame of beache wth fower turned postes," and also "three billyard stickes and 11 balles of yvery"; and in the same year the Earl of Leicester's goods at Wanstead, as listed for probate, included "a billiarde table with the tools appurteyninge." [13] Other country-house billiard rooms which available information indicates are both original and early include those at Burghley House (completed 1589), Bramshill (completed 1612), Knole (completed 1608), Dorton House (completed 1626), and Hatfield House (completed 1611).[14]

Although the billiard room was as richly appointed as any other in the country house—with, for example, paintings by such artists as Holbein, Canaletto, and Van Dyck—the table itself was often an object of great interest to visitor and owner alike. Thus John Evelyn, in his seventeenth-century diary, carefully noted the billiard tables in the houses he visited. In 1844 the Duke of Devonshire proudly described his table at Chatsworth as follows:

> The Billiard-table, made by Thurston, full size—which means that there is still a fuller size—is suited to the smallness of the room. . . . The table, of birds-eye maple, is a chef d'oeuvre of workmanship, and has been

[12] But cf. James Gibbs, *A Book of Architecture containing Designs of Buildings and Ornaments,* 2d ed. (London: W. Innys and R. Manby, 1739), p. xiii and plate XLVIII.

[13] Quoted from "Tables, Billiard," in Ralph Edwards (Ed.), *Dictionary of English Furniture,* 2d ed. (London: Country Life, 1954), pp. 187 ff.; this article is in every respect the best account of early billiard history in England. Note that these 1588 quotations slightly antedate the *O.E.D.*'s first record of the word "billiards" in the English language (1591).

[14] Anon., *Guide to Burghley House, Stamford* (Stamford: Doby Brothers, 1933), p. 19; William Cope, *Bramshill: Its History and Architecture* (London: H. J. Infield, n.d. [after 1875]), p. 36; H. Avray Tipping, *English Homes: Late Tudor and Early Stuart, 1558–1649* (London: Country Life, 1929), p. 246; James Hakewell, *An Attempt to Determine the Exact Character of Elizabethan Architecture,* 2d ed. (London: John Weale, 1936), p. [30]; Robert Kerr, *The Gentleman's House,* 3rd ed. (London: John Murray, 1871), plate 9.

pronounced excellent by no less a man than "Jonathan" [a famous player of the time].[15]

Among the prize-winning examples of English craftsmanship at the Great Exhibition of 1851 were two billiard tables (by different manufacturers) with elaborate marquetry and other ornamentation.[16]

By the time of Robert Kerr's *The Gentleman's House; Or, How to Plan English Residences* (first edition, 1864; third edition, 1871), it was taken for granted that any house of reasonable size should have a billiard room, and Kerr devoted a good deal of attention to the matter.[17] So did some of the Victorian manuals on billiards.[18]

From the beginning, billiard tables also were installed in some other meeting places of the upper class. Most important of these, perhaps, were the two billiard tables in the New Assembly Rooms at Bath (built 1769–1771).[19] Some upper-class coffee houses also had billiard tables—starting with Colsini's Chocolate House, which had two billiard tables by 1693, and ending with the Smyrna Coffee House in St James's Street,

[15] Anon. [Duke of Devonshire], *Handbook of Chatsworth and Hardwick* (London: Privately printed, n.d. [1844]), p. 35.

[16] Color lithographs of these tables comprise plate 190 of the exhibition catalogue. Among the more notable English tables preserved is the present one at Burghley House, whose mountings are of oak from the Royal George, sunk at Spithead in 1782. A table from about 1660, now in the Victoria and Albert Museum, is illustrated in Ralph Edwards, *op. cit.* Probably the oldest English table extant is the one at Knole. It is illustrated in Tipping, *op. cit.,* and Edwards, *op. cit.;* its construction is briefly discussed in Margaret Jourdain, *Stuart Furniture at Knole* (London: Country Life, 1952), p. 13. Edwards, following Tipping, dates it around 1690, but I think Jourdain correctly dates the base of it about a century earlier.

[17] The construction of billiard rooms in English country houses continued well into the present century. For photographs of billiard rooms in houses not already cited, consult the files of *Country Life* and also Charles Latham's *In English Homes* (London: Country Life) as follows: Vol. 1 (1904), pp. 24, 56, 348, 365, 405; Vol. 2 (1907), pp. 166, 359, 431; Vol. 3 (1909), pp. 412, 414.

[18] See especially the lovely architectural elevations for Greek Revival and Tudor billiard annexes attached to mansions, in William Dufton's *Practical Billiards* (London: George Routledge, 1873), plates 2, 3, 4, and 5.

[19] See the floor plan in Mowbray A. Green, *The Eighteenth Century Architecture of Bath* (Bath: George Gregory, 1904), p. 161.

which advertised itself in 1801 as a place where "Gentlemen meet on purpose to play billiards." [20]

But if billiards could be played in public places frequented by gentlemen, there was little to prevent it being played in public places frequented by the not-so-gentlemanly; and little did prevent it. This newer type of English billiard playing, which represented a "trickling down" of the upper-class pastime, appears to have been already well under way in the seventeenth century, to judge from Charles Cotton's remarks of 1674:

> The Gentile, cleanly and most ingenious game at Billiards . . . is much approved of and played by most Nations in *Europe,* especially in *England* there being few Towns of note therein which hath not a publick Billiard-table, neither are they wanting in many Noble and private Families in the Country.[21]

As this second tradition developed, the "respectable" upper class who played at home or in meeting places restricted to their own kind (Bath, private clubs, etc.) were immediately concerned to distinguish themselves from it, and in doing so they conceived it as morally deviant. In their view, it was bad enough that *hoi aristoi* had occasionally spent too much time and money gambling at billiards among themselves (Edmund Spenser's complaint of 1591),[22] but much worse that *hoi polloi* should now become wastrels over it and even (worst of all) sometimes seduce their weaker-minded betters into joining with them in a life of dissolute gaming. That is why even as early as 1674 Charles Cotton, for all his remarks about "The Gentile, cleanly and most ingenious game at Billiards," had to leaven his book with remarks such as these:

> Mistake me not, it is not my intention to make Gamesters.

[20] Cf. Bryant Lillywhite, *London Coffee Houses* (London: George Allen and Unwin, 1963), entries numbered 7, 500, 1178, 1223, and 1604.

[21] Gamester [Charles Cotton], *The compleat Gamester; or, Instructions how to play at billiards, trucks, bowls and chess. . . .* (London: Henry Brome, 1674), p. 23.

[22] "With all the thriftless games that may be found. . . . With dice, with cards, with billiards." *Mother Hubberd's Tale* (1591).

This restless man (the miserable Gamester) is the proper subject of every man's pity. Restless I call him, because (such is the itch of play) either winning or losing he can never be satisfied, if he wins he thinks to win more, if he loses he hopes to recover.

To conclude, let me advise you, if you play (when your business will permit) let not a covetous desire of winning another's money engage you to the losing of your own.[23]

As billiards spread downward from the upper class, these kinds of warnings increased in frequency and severity. There were also occasional efforts to go beyond moral suasion and legally clamp down on public billiard playing by the lower strata, such as this attempt in the Dublin of 1744:

At the Court of *King's Bench,* in *Ireland,* were convicted 15 of the Billiard Tables, presented by the Grand Jury of *Dublin,* (who had traversed) The Citizens have determin'd to prosecute, in the same Manner, all Billiard Tables that shall be erected for the Future, or those which now remain, if kept open after 9 o'Clock at Night, or knowingly suffer Merchants, Apprentices or Clerks belonging to Gentlemen of any Business, to play in their Houses.[24]

These attempts, whether in England or Ireland, succeeded only rarely and temporarily. But in any case there had developed, in addition to the approved "gentleman's game" played in country houses, public billiard playing by non-gentlemen that was heavily stigmatized.]

IV

[In America as in England, billiards began at the top. It came as a direct importation from the English upper class to the American upper class. For example, one of the earliest genuine references to billiards in America reveals that the Colonial

[23] Charles Cotton, *op. cit.,* pp. [vi], [vii–viii], 3.
[24] "Historical Chronicle," *Gentleman's Magazine,* Vol. 14 (1744), p. 337.

statesman William Byrd of Westover—who was educated in
England and called to the bar at the Middle Temple—had a
billiard table: in his diary entry for 30 July 1710, Byrd writes,
apropos of having laid his wife, "It is to be observed that the
flourish was performed on the billiard table." [25] On September
26, 1725, I find the Colonial Governor of New York, George
Clinton, writing to Cadwallader Colden that "I . . . gave orders
for my Billiard tables to be Set up." [26] By 1768, according to
an account written in that year, the demand for billiard playing
equipment was already so great that cue sticks manufactured
along the James River in Virginia were being exported all the
way to Boston.[27] (Despite sharply increasing demand over the
next 150 years, this early American industry died out in Virginia, presumably because of the realization that the most warp-
resistant woods for cue sticks are the extremely hard varieties of
maple which flourish much further north.[28])

The better-off merchant of the times could avail himself of
such offerings as this one in the New York *Royal Gazette* of
October 24, 1781:

To be let a new house in an excellent stand for business,

[25] Cf. Louis B. Wright and Marion Tinling (Eds.), *Secret Diary of
William Byrd of Westover, 1709–1712* (Richmond, Va.; Dietz Press,
1941), p. 207.

[26] Cf. *Letters and Papers of Cadwallader Colden.* Vol. IX: *Additional Letters and Papers, 1749–1775* (New York: New York Historical
Society, 1937), p. 122.

[27] Cf. *Virginia Gazette,* March 3, 1768, p. 3, col. 1.

[28] Cue sticks are usually 56½ to 57 inches long, the better ones
being take-down models comprising two pieces of equal length, a butt
and a shaft, joined via an inset brass female screw in the bottom of the
shaft and a brass male screw and bushing in the top of the butt. The
relatively thick butt can be made of any of various heavy woods (e.g.,
my own is of West African black ebony) and traditionally has a good
deal of marquetry using inlays of ivory, colored woods, and mother-of-
pearl. But the shaft, since it tapers to a width of only 12½ to
13½ millimeters throughout the last several inches of its length, must,
if it is to resist warping, be an unadorned piece of very hard maple,
turned so that the grain runs straight down the shaft, from stock that
has been thoroughly kiln-dried. To produce maple shafts that are all
of first quality—a criterion ignored by the newer stickmakers—one
must also take care to use only the heartwood near the center of the
log (for which last information I am indebted to the best of the old
cue-stick craftsmen, octogenarian Herman Rambow of Chicago).

it has a good cellar, two rooms below, a large billiard room above, a bed chamber, a large garret, a back kitchen, and a convenient back yard. . . .

And early American newspapers also contain quite a few advertisements addressed to the upper class along the lines of this one from the *Minerva & Mercantile Advertiser* of February 12, 1795:

William King, Ivory and Wood Turner, Informs the citizens . . . that he has commenced the turning business. . . . Billiard balls made at the shortest notice . . .

Upper-class billiard playing long survived the Colonial era. For instance, the education typically given a scion of wealth in the mid-nineteenth century was described accurately, albeit sarcastically, by Charles Nordhoff in 1868 as follows:

J. Augustus . . . was of course in due time sent to college, where he acquired the proper proficiency in Greek, Latin, and Mathematics, slang, billiards, and brandy smashes.[29]

In fact, the British tradition of upper-class participation in billiards has in America had a continuous, if latterly rather modest, history.[30] A good many illustrious Americans have played billiards. And today the members of the Billiard Room Proprietors Association and the Billiard Congress of America tirelessly cite such personages in the hope that this will improve their "image." But their hope is misplaced, for they thoroughly misunderstand the relation of billiards to upper-class life.

In the first place, genteel upper-class billiard playing in America, as in England, was insulated from the rest of society,

[29] Charles Nordhoff, "Maud Elbert's Love Match," in his *Cape Cod and All Along the Shore: Stories* (New York: Harper and Brothers, 1868), p. 217.

[30] See especially the house organs and archives of upper-class men's clubs with billiard rooms. The first national amateur billiard tournament was organized by the Racquet and Tennis Club of New York in 1887. A good account of the billiard enthusiasts in nineteenth-century clubland is A. L. Ranney, M.D., "A Historical Sketch of Amateur Billiards," in *Amateur Billiard Championship of America* (*Class A*)—*Souvenir of the First Tournament Given Under the Auspices of the Amateur Athletic Union of the United States* (New York: Knickerbocker Athletic Club, 1899), pp. 7–24.

and its rise and fall have followed a dynamic of their own. What professional players and poolroom owners conveniently ignore is that "the gentleman's game," to the extent that gentlemen really played it, throughout its history has had precious little to do with public poolrooms, but instead has been restricted to the billiard rooms of private men's clubs and private homes.[31] And the upper class knows what this means even if the professionals don't. The point of the remark falsely attributed to Herbert Spencer, "To play a good game of billiards is the sign of a well-rounded education, but to play too good a game of billiards is the sign of a mis-spent youth," is precisely the point made in that *locus classicus* for the ideology of the "gentleman," Lord Chesterfield's letters to his son, when Chesterfield warns his son against becoming too good a flute player: the upper class must uphold the distinction between the amateur and the professional, and the true gentleman takes care that he cannot possibly be mistaken for a professional or vice versa.

This moral has never been lost on the American billiard-playing elite, and the traditional attempts of professional pool and billiard players to identify themselves with such circles, e.g., by wearing tuxedos when appearing in professional tournaments, are merely pathetic. To be sure, a Luther Lassiter or a Willie Mosconi may be invited to give an exhibition before the assembled members of a men's club—a comedown from the days when Willie Hoppe gave command performances for presidents and royalty, but still something. And if the profes-

---

[31] For one of the more interesting examples in the American private home, see the photograph of the billiard room designed about 1900 by Louis Tiffany for his country estate, The Briars, Long Island, in Robert Koch, *Louis C. Tiffany: Rebel in Glass* (New York: Crown Publishers, 1964), p. 183. See also C. V. Boyd, "Billiard Room of a Country House," *Suburban Life,* Vol. 18 (January 1914), pp. 10–12. [The earliest surviving billiard table of American manufacture, made in Maryland between 1790 and 1810, is in the Winterthur Museum.] A picture of it, and background information, are in Louise C. Belden, "Billiards in America Before 1830," *Antiques,* Vol. 87, No. 1 (January 1965), pp. 99–101. Miss Belden's is easily the best writing on its subject heretofore published, but is more restricted than its title indicates: it deals exclusively with upper-class billiard history, and in a limited way (e.g., using none of the pre-1830 material from the upper class that I have quoted).

sional should need money in his later years he may even end his days in their permanent employ (e.g., the old balk-line billiard champion Jake Schaefer, Jr., has for some time run the billiard room of the Cleveland Athletic Club). But it is all part of the relation of master to hired performer. Even Willie Hoppe, who was a real stuffed shirt and tried his damnedest to dissociate himself from the poolroom subculture (he didn't even smoke or drink), for all his wealth and gentlemanly yearnings and polite manners never quite made it in the upper class as an equal.

In the past, major poolrooms did indeed manage to attract some upper-class patrons, not only *nouveaux riches* businessmen but occasional scions of old wealthy families as well. However, such people were a different breed from the gentlemen who played at the Union League or at home over cigars and sherry, and in fact comprised the most disreputable segment of the upper class. One of the latent functions of the American poolroom, like the racetrack in many of its phases, was as a place where the "sporting" fringe of the upper class—the hedonists and hellraisers given to heavy drinking and gambling and whoring—could get together with the "sporting element" of the lower class and lower-middle class to the exclusion of those who subscribed to "middle-class morality." [32] Poolrooms were major gathering places for the sporting fraternity and served them in various ways; e.g., in the early 1920's, Jack Doyle's Billiard Academy was the place where the daily "line" (more or less official bookmakers' odds) was determined for every sports event in New York City.[33]

---

[32] For example, see the further remarks of Keogh in Russell Phillips, *op. cit.*, p. 15. Public billiard rooms in England of course had a similar function; cf. Edward Russell Mardon, *Billiards: Game 500 Up. Played at Brighton, on the 18th of January, 1844. A Description of the Above Game, with Diagrams Shewing the Position of the Balls for the Last Nine Breaks* (Brighton: W. Leppard, n.d. [1844]), pp. 4, 102–103.

[33] For this information on Doyle's Academy I am indebted to my father, Joseph Polsky.

V

What used to be called "sporting life," the orientation of leisure around a set of hedonistic and deviant concerns, has in America not died out or even diminished. Rather, it has retained many of its old institutional forms (bookies and racetracks, orgies and stag shows, after-hours liquor-cum-gambling joints, cocaine, bars where prostitutes are permitted or encouraged to operate, floating crap and card games), while sloughing off some others (poolrooms, whorehouses, opium, burlesque houses) and developing some new ones (call-girl organizations operating through model agencies and escort services, marihuana, the gambling centers of Lake Tahoe and Las Vegas, free-lance call girls operating via telephone-answering services, phenomenally increased gambling at golf). It remains to be explained why poolrooms got lost in the shuffle.

One answer sometimes given, and at first glance an appealing one, has to do not with the poolroom's latent functions but its manifest functions: a place where one plays or watches pool and billiards. It is occasionally said that pool and billiards were killed by other sports, especially the rise of mass participation in bowling and mass spectatorship for professional football.

It has been claimed apropos of the first that, relative to bowling, pool and billiards are too hard to learn well. The argument goes that thousands of regular bowlers can work up to an average of 180 or better, but that getting to the point in pool where you can average nearly 10 balls an inning and occasionally run more than 50, or to the point in three-cushion billiards where you can average 1 an inning and occasionally run more than 7, is a very much more difficult matter.

There are some genuine grains of truth at the bottom of this argument. Outstanding pool or billiard play requires thousands of hours of practice, and, to boot, early entry, as much as outstanding piano playing does. I have never met or heard of a really first-class pool or billiard player who was not playing regularly by his early teens. An additional fact supporting this position, though it seems never to have been adduced, is that many of the greatest pool and billiard players, probably the majority, started training well before their teens because they were sons of poolroom owners (e.g., Ralph Greenleaf, Willie Hoppe, Babe Cranfield, Jay Bozeman, Willie Mosconi, Welker Cochran) and in one case the son of a professional player (Jake Schaefer, Jr.). But this entire line of argument really doesn't hold up, for it assumes that true enjoyment of the game depends on attaining to the level of the top one-fifth of 1 per cent of players. The fact is that millions of Americans have greatly enjoyed playing pool regularly even though they have never come close to running 50 balls—have enjoyed it just as much as, say, the millions of golfers who have never broken 80 have enjoyed playing golf. And as we saw earlier, in the 1850's billiards in fact superseded bowling in popularity; there seems to be no reason intrinsic to these games themselves why such a reversal couldn't happen again.]

The second point of view sees a shift in spectator sports interests as perhaps the chief villain in the piece.[For example, Willie Mosconi has recalled that, in Chicago in the early 1930's, it was common for him to draw 1500 spectators to a Saturday night pool exhibition while the Chicago Bears would draw 1200 the next day.[34] It is undeniably true that from about 1930 on poolrooms steadily declined while, during the depression era, spectator interest in football, basketball, etc., began to rise; and it is also true that as the depression eased, most depression-hurt sports made recoveries but pool and billiards declined very much more. However, there is no evidence of a real cause-and-effect relationship here. Pool and billiards have always had plenty of competition for spectators (and players) from any number of other sports and games, and did quite well nonetheless.]

Similarly, it is illogical to blame the decline of poolrooms on the spread of radios, automobiles, and the movies.[35] There is

[34] Cf. Mosconi as quoted in the New York *Post,* December 18, 1961, p. 62.

[35] As, for example, Robert Coughlan does in his "Pool: Its Players and Its Sharks," *Life,* Vol. 31, No. 15 (October 8, 1951), p. 166.

no evidence whatsoever that their negative effect on poolroom attendance was any greater than that provided by the many popular diversions which existed in the palmy days of the poolroom (such as the home phonograph and player piano, vaudeville and the legitimate theatre, public dance halls and ballrooms, taverns, racetracks, and so on).

And if mass spectatorship for sports has any relevance as such, then the post-1945 role of television in fantastically increasing that spectatorship should, if anything, have helped pool and billiards even more than most other sports. For a pool or billiard game is ideal for TV: it is not as spread out and hard to follow on television as football or baseball, and when the camera looks down on the table from a reasonably steep angle (as it usually does), the home viewer gets a truer picture of the game than even the front-row spectators do. Yet television did nothing to revive pool and billiards; such games did not become TV fare until mid-1963, after the revival was well under way.

Finally, one should note that although the current poolroom revival is already exhibiting danger signs (more on this below), the sale of small-sized pool tables to homeowners is still sharply increasing. The ups and downs of poolrooms, as we shall see, have had not so much to do with pool as with poolrooms.

VI

As we have observed, the various alleged "causes" for the decay of the American poolroom have had a minor role at best. The genuine prime cause seems never to have been mentioned: poolrooms were the exact center and veritable stronghold of a special kind of subculture that has become increasingly rare and unimportant in America—the heterosexual but all-male subculture, which required that certain gathering places (clubs, barber shops, taverns) serve as sacrosanct refuges from women. The poolroom was not just one of these places: it was *the* one, the keystone.

The once-great attraction of pool and billiards, both for spectators and players, was in large part factitious; it had not so much to do with the games themselves as with the poolroom's latent function as the greatest and most determinedly all-male institution in American social life. The poolroom got so thoroughly bound up with this function that it could not readily adapt itself to changed conditions; when the subculture died, the poolroom nearly died with it.

To see the true dimensions of this historical drift, one must realize that the old poolroom depended not merely, or even primarily, on the equivalent of today's audience of unmarried teenagers combined with husbands out for a weekly "night with the boys" or playing at lunchtime, but on people who spent far more time than these in the poolroom: adult men who were heterosexual but nevertheless committed to remaining unmarried. Moreover, the ideology of this bachelor subculture spilled over to married life itself; i.e., married men spent more nights "out with the boys" than they do today, which of course further helped poolroom attendance. (Both the "pure" and the "married" subcultural types linger in the nation's historical consciousness, or nostalgia, via highly anachronistic comic-strip characters; Moon Mullins pre-eminently represents the first type, while the second is notably represented by Mutt and Major Hoople.)

As everyone appears to know thanks to Kinsey, if an American male over the age of 35 has never been married there is a strong chance that he is actively and primarily homosexual.[36] But what everyone seems to forget is that this is a major change in the odds and represents a recent shift in America's sexual history. For various reasons connected with our country's economic development and its historic patterns of immigration, not

---

[36] Among unmarried American males 35 or older with at least a ninth-grade education, about 42 per cent have at least as much homosexual experience per year as heterosexual experience; among those with less than a ninth-grade education, about 28 per cent have at least as much homosexual experience per year as heterosexual experience. Cf. Alfred Kinsey, Wardell Pomeroy, and Clyde Martin, *Sexual Behavior in the Human Male* (Philadelphia: W. B. Saunders Co., 1948), p. 644, fig. 164.

too long ago the heterosexual confirmed bachelor was a common American social type. For example, the bachelor "uncle" —sometimes a real uncle, sometimes an honorary one, but in any event a bachelor—was a fixture in hundreds of thousands of American families. He may not have been very active sexually, but his sexual activity, such as it was, was rarely homosexual. (I am talking about overt behavior only; what existed in repressed form may be another story.) His sexual needs were met throughout his life partly by masturbation and partly or mainly by regular recourse to professional whores. Today American men use whores pre-maritally, extra-maritally, and post-maritally, but hardly ever any more as a way of maintaining lifelong bachelorhood.[37]

Curiously, American historians seem never to have assayed, indeed to be oblivious of, the swiftly growing role of a confirmed-bachelor subculture in the social history of nineteenth-century America. Yet the evidence is plain enough.

For one thing, a number of American institutions whose palmy days were in the later nineteenth or early twentieth century immediately reveal themselves, once their histories are examined, as having drawn sustenance from that subculture and often, indeed, having been part and parcel of it—not only the poolroom, but institutions as various as the I.W.W., lodges and other fraternal organizations, red-light districts, middle-class and upper-class men's clubs, tramp and hobo life. Secondly, there increasingly emerged, in the lowbrow and middlebrow literature of the times, much that gave bachelors a consciousness of kind and gave ideological expression to permanent bachelorhood (as in the *Police Gazette,* whose formerly vital role in our popular culture is hard to appreciate now). Thirdly, the most sophisticated compilation of historical statistics on

[37] In this connection note the Kinsey data, which reveal that although the percentage of males born after 1900 who visited prostitutes was not significantly different from the percentage among males born earlier, the frequency with which they made such visits had been reduced to about half what it was in the pre-1900 generation. Cf. Alfred Kinsey, Wardell Pomeroy, Clyde Martin, and Paul Gebhard, *Sexual Behavior in the Human Female* (Philadelphia: W. B. Saunders Co., 1953), p. 300.

American marriage—the work of Paul Jacobson—reveals the
early American rate of permanent bachelorhood to have been
a steadily rising one that peaked during the lifetimes of the men
born around 1865–1870 (i.e., men just entering their adulthood in the late 1880's and early 1890's). Jacobson's cohort
analyses of bachelors and spinsters (single whites aged 15 and
over) from successive decades of the late eighteenth century
through the nineteenth century show that

> there was a gradual decrease in the proportion ultimately
> marrying among persons born in successive periods up
> to the years immediately after the Civil War, and there-
> after a gradual increase.

Jacobson notes further that

> the marriage rate for bachelors and spinsters has gener-
> ally moved upward during this century. Among single
> men, for example, the average annual marriage rate rose
> from 64 per 1,000 in the 1900's to 69 in the 1920's.
> Although the rate dropped sharply during the depression
> of the 1930's, it soared upward in the next decade to
> the unusually high level of 92 per 1,000.
>   Another indication of the increased propensity to
> marry is afforded by the extent to which the single popu-
> lation has been depleted. Among males aged 15 and
> over (including those in the armed forces overseas) the
> proportion single declined from 42 percent in 1890 . . .
> to less than 25 per cent in 1950.[38]

VII

Toward the middle of the nineteenth century, hard upon
the great waves of Irish and German immigration, the American
poolroom began to emerge as the major physical locus of the
rising bachelor subculture. One witness to the start of the boom
wrote as follows in 1850:

[38] Paul Jacobson, *American Marriage and Divorce* (New York:
Rinehart, 1959), p. 35. For additional details, see especially Tables 7
and 8, pp. 34–35. The paragraphs above assess fully neither the heterosexual bachelor subculture nor its former place in American life, but
attempt merely to indicate that such assessment is a desideratum in
American historiography.

The rapidity with which Billiard rooms have increased in this and other cities of the Union, is extraordinary. Within the writer's memory, the number of rooms in New York, did not exceed seven or eight, and perhaps not more than sixteen tables in all; now, there are from fifty to sixty rooms, with a number of tables, varying from one to sixteen each, and amounting, on the whole, to something over four hundred.[39]

The periodical of the time most concerned with "popular culture," *Frank Leslie's Illustrated Newspaper,* in January 1859 began a regular column on billiards. April of the same year saw the first thing approximating a national championship contest, the Phelan-Seereiter match in Detroit.[40] The popularity that the sport had already gained is indicated by the fact that this match, the first professional billiard event for which admission was charged, was a sellout at the high admission price of $5, was played for the enormous prize of $15,000 (surely over $100,000 in today's currency), and was altogether one of the most gripping events on the American "sporting imagination" of the nineteenth century. *The New York Times'* coverage of the match—this when the whole newspaper was only eight to twelve pages—appears in several columns over three separate issues. In 1865 the periodical *Round Table* took note of "the

[39] Michael Phelan, *Billiards Without a Master* (New York: D. D. Winant, 1850), p. 122. This, the first American book on billiards, went into several editions. Phelan also issued the first American billiard periodical, *Billiard Cue,* from 1856 to 1874; it was a monthly of four folio pages. Cf. Frank Luther Mott, *A History of American Magazines, 1850–1865* (Cambridge, Mass.: Harvard University Press, 1938), p. 203.

[40] The names of the contestants are significant. In keeping with ethnic shifts in American immigration, most of the early non-WASP billiard professionals are of Irish origin (Phelan, Daly, Kavanagh, Gallagher, Keogh, McKenna, *et al.*) or of German origin (Seereiter, Schaefer, Kieckhefer, Reiselt, Hoppe, *et al.*), with Italians and Jews becoming prominent in the picture only after the turn of the century.

The heavy extent to which German-Americans were involved in billiards has been overlooked by billiard historians, probably because the first American billiard books were written by Irishmen, but there is much evidence apart from the names of early professionals. For example, in the middle of the nineteenth century a number of the German beer gardens along the Bowery in New York City had billiard tables. Cf. Matthew Hale Smith, *Sunshine and Shadow in New York* (Hartford, Conn.: J. B. Burr, 1869), p. 216.

mania for playing billiards which has developed itself in this country in the last five or six years." [41]

The swift increase noted at mid-century was a mere beginning. The pace of poolroom growth accelerated throughout the second half of the nineteenth century and well into the twentieth. By the mid-1920's America had over 42,000 poolrooms (over 4,000 in New York City alone), many with more than 50 tables each and even a few with 100 tables each.[42] Detroit Recreation, a poolroom in Detroit that claimed to be the world's largest, had 125 tables. In the 1920's, Ralph Greenleaf, the greatest pool champion in the history of the game, played the Palace Theatre at a salary of $2,000 per week. And note what happened to one of the instruction manuals, *Daly's Billiard Book,* which was published in 1913: in its first ten years, it achieved a larger sale than any other book devoted to a physical sport or game that had ever been published.[43]

The timing of all this is significant beyond the fact of bachelorhood *per se.* It is not accidental that poolrooms began rapidly to increase in number and size as the American frontier rapidly receded, for one function of the frontier was as a male

[41] Quoted in Mott, *op. cit.,* p. 203.

[42] Statistics on the number of poolrooms, put out from time to time by such organizations as the Billiard Congress of America, National Billiard Council, and Billiard Room Proprietors Association of America, vary considerably. The consensus seems to be that in 1964 there were 11,000 poolrooms, up more than 3,000 from 1960. Estimates of the peak number of poolrooms in the 1920's vary between 40,000 and 45,000, with 42,000 the most frequently used figure. Estimates of the peak number of poolrooms in New York City in the 1920's range from 4,000 to 5,000; according to reporter Robert Deasy (*World Telegram & Sun,* June 24, 1963), in 1961 New York City had only 257 licensed poolrooms with a total of 2,177 tables and in 1962 (after the revival had begun) had 291 poolrooms with 2,504 tables. According to Dixie Dean Harris (*Pageant,* August, 1964, p. 114), Detroit had a thousand poolrooms in the 1920's but only 156 poolrooms in 1964. Robert Coughlan (*op. cit.,* p. 166) estimates that the number of pool and billiard tables in use had declined from over 500,000 in the 1920's to only one-fifth that number in 1951. Although these and other published statistics permit of no exact agreement, the enormous magnitude of the decline from the 1920's is clear enough in all of them.

[43] Cf. Maurice Daly, *Daly's Billiard Book,* 6th ed., (Chicago: A. C. McClurg & Co., 1923), p. [viii].

escape-hatch from effete and "feminized" urban civilization.[44] As towns and cities spread ever westward and as they more and more "settled down," the poolroom blossomed as a kind of behind-the-lines or inner frontier, the new no-woman's land, catering to internal refugees from the world of female-imposed gentility, catering to men who wanted to be able to curse and spit tobacco, fight freely, dress sloppily, gamble heavily, get roaring drunk, whore around.

Nor is it accidental that Mark Twain, the American author we most associate with chafing at his entrapment in the respectability of urban civilization and with nostalgic longing for woman-free frontier days, should of all American authors be the one most truly to fall in love with billiard playing and poolroom life.[45] Nor is it accidental that the poolroom and the heterosexual bachelor disappear simultaneously from the American landscape (which is why not the depression, but the easing of the depression was the real death-knell of the poolroom). Nor is it accidental that the most regular and devoted of today's poolroom spectators, the old men who come day after day and use the poolroom as a poor man's club, consist overwhelmingly of old-style bachelors and once-bitten-twice-shy widowers. Nor, finally, is it accidental that the most regular and devoted of today's poolroom players, the pool and billiard hustlers who virtually live in the poolroom and build their very careers around poolroom life, comprise one of the last American occupational groups in which the majority of adults are non-homosexual bachelors.

[44] Awareness of this role of the frontier runs through much of early American literature; cf. Leslie Fiedler, *Love and Death in the American Novel* (New York: Criterion Books, 1960), *passim.*

[45] Cf. William Dean Howells, "My Memories of Mark Twain," *Harper's Monthly Magazine,* Vol. 121 (July 1910), pp. 170–71; Albert Bigelow Paine, *Mark Twain: A Biography* (New York: Harper and Brothers, 1912), Vol. 2, pp. 613–14, and Vol. 3, pp. 1324–32, 1366–70; Willie Hoppe, *Thirty Years of Billiards* (New York: G. P. Putnam's, 1925), pp. 109–114, 117. According to Hoppe, Twain attended every big billiard match in New York for years. From Paine's account, especially pp. 613–14, it appears that Twain used his own billiard playing as a means of getting together with male cronies to the exclusion of his wife and daughter.

VIII

As Friedrich Nietzsche first observed, an institution when deprived of its major function does not *eo ipso* go out of business, but often survives and prospers by taking on new functions.[46] Modern sociology, with its studies of the changing role of the family, the church, the settlement house, etc., has abundantly confirmed Nietzsche's insight. Might not the poolroom in this way flourish once more—by redefining itself as a place "for the family" and catering to women as well as men, as indeed most new-look poolrooms are trying to do? In theory, yes; in practice, no. An institution that tries to change its function sometimes fails, and this appears to be the poolroom's fate. Of course, poolrooms will not cease to exist, and their number may even increase a bit over the next few years, but there are several reasons why "cleaning up the game" and changing its "image" so as to attract women will never restore to poolrooms anything remotely like the degree of popularity they once had.

Bringing women in—with the attendant paraphernalia of free instruction for them, special women's tournaments, the curbing of obscenity and other loutish male behavior so that women will feel comfortable, etc.—has been tried several times before.[47] Each time it has had a modicum of initial success and then died. This is only to be expected.

Granted three notable exceptions—the billiard player May Kaarlus around the turn of the century, the pool player Ruth McGinnis in the 1930's, and the billiard player Masako Katsura today—poolroom games pose near-insuperable problems for women. First, male-female differences in the structure of the arm affect development of a good stroke, making it very difficult for a woman to become good at these games relative to

[46] Cf. Section XII of " 'Guilt,' 'Bad Conscience,' and the Like," *Genealogy of Morals.*

[47] For example, see *Billiards Magazine* (June, 1932), pp. 6–9. See also "Swank Pool Hall Attracts Women of Springfield, Ill.," *Life,* Vol. 23 (November 17, 1947), pp. 71–72; the poolroom described in this article later went out of business.

other games (just as a woman can, if she is athletically inclined, become a good bowler or underhand softball pitcher but can never learn to throw a ball overhand very well). Secondly, many shots require leaning way over the table or even putting one leg up on the table, involving a display of legs (if a skirt is worn) or buttocks (if slacks are worn) that most women find quite embarrassing. Thirdly and most importantly, there are the kind of teenage boys and men who hang around poolrooms. No poolroom proprietor can completely curb their profanity, leering, attempts to pick up the women. Nor can he really get rid of them, for the simple reason that they comprise the great bulk of his business.

That last point is crucial. For nearly all the women who play, it is a passing fad, something that lately *Mademoiselle* and *Vogue* and even *Saturday Evening Post* have told them is "in" but that is forgotten when the next new kick comes along. For the reasons just stated, women almost never stick with poolroom games; they soon tend to visit the poolroom infrequently or drop out completely, whereas the men are far more likely to be or become regular players.[48] And the new-style poolrooms hopeful of catering to women are quickly finding this out. Once the initial novelty has worn off, the proprietor finds that his trade consists mostly of teenage boys, especially the school dropouts, and secondarily the old-style "sporting" types among the adult males. They play so much oftener and longer than women or teenage girls that he can't afford to kick them out.

[48] Private (non-poolroom) playing by the upper class, which I have not tried to discuss in detail in this study, shows a different pattern of female participation. Although women were of course excluded from playing at men's clubs, the attitude toward their playing at home varied at different times and places; sometimes the home billiard room was an exclusively male preserve, but usually women were also allowed to play, and often did so. Thus Robert Kerr advised that the home billiard room should "be situated not exactly amongst the Dwelling-rooms, but still in close connection with them, for the access of the ladies" (Kerr, *op. cit.,* 3rd ed., p. 120). Women playing billiards at home are shown in many British and American engravings of the eighteenth and nineteenth centuries, e.g., in Rowlandson's "The Billiard Table" (1820) from his *Dr. Syntax* series. This tradition of upper-class female billiard playing has few exemplars today, the most notable being the Queen Mother of England.

Many of the new poolrooms are doing good business, notably those in postwar population centers that never had poolrooms before. The revival has indeed found enough of a market to support such places. But already the cream has been skimmed off this market. Already a number of poolrooms that opened with the fanciest of intentions now must rely on clientele who are anything but fancy; e.g., one suburban poolroom that two years ago received acres of publicity about its "respectability" is now a center of narcotics distribution. Already, in every section of the country, the rate at which new poolrooms are opening is going down. Already many of the snazzy new poolrooms are in financial trouble, falling behind in their payments to the equipment manufacturers. And that's with only about a fourth as many poolrooms as America had when its population was little over half what it is now. The heyday of the poolroom is over.

2
The Hustler*

Such a man spends all his life playing every day for small stakes. Give him every morning the money that he may gain during the day, on condition that he does not play—you will make him unhappy. It will perhaps be said that what he seeks is the amusement of play, not gain. Let him play then for nothing; he will lose interest and be wearied.—*Blaise Pascal*

They talk about me not being on the legitimate. Why, lady, nobody's on the legit when it comes down to cases; you know that.—*Al Capone* [1]

The poolroom hustler makes his living by betting against his opponents in different types of pool or billiard games, and as part of the playing and betting process he engages in various deceitful practices. The terms "hustler" for such a person and "hustling" for his occupation have been in poolroom argot for decades, antedating their application to prostitutes. Usually the hustler plays with his own money, but often he makes use of a "backer." In the latter event the standard arrangement is that the backer, in return for assuming all risk of loss, receives half of the hustler's winnings.

The hustler's offense in the eyes of many is not that he breaks misdemeanor laws against gambling (perhaps most Americans have done so at one time or another), but that he does so daily. Also—and again as a necessary and regular part of his daily work—he violates American norms concerning (a) what is morally correct behavior toward one's fellow man and (b) what is a proper and fitting occupation. For one or an-

---

* Approximately the first third of this chapter appeared, in slightly different form, in *Social Problems,* Vol. 12, No. 1 (Summer, 1964), pp. 3–15.

[1] The Pascal quotation is from *Pensées,* V. Al Capone's remark is quoted in Paul Sann, *The Lawless Decade* (New York: Crown Publishers, 1957), p. 214.

other of these related reasons the hustler is stigmatized by respectable outsiders. The most knowledgeable of such outsiders see the hustler not merely as a gambler but as one who violates an ethic of fair dealing; they regard him as a criminal or quasi-criminal not because he gambles but because he systematically "victimizes" people. Somewhat less knowledgeable outsiders put down the hustler simply because gambling is his trade. Still less knowledgeable outsiders (perhaps the majority) regard hustlers as persons who, whatever they may actually do, certainly do not hold down visibly respectable jobs; therefore this group also stigmatizes hustlers—"poolroom bums" is the classic phrase—and believes that society would be better' off without them. Hustling, to the degree that it is known to the larger society at all, is classed with that large group of social problems composed of morally deviant occupations.

However, in what follows I try to present hustlers and hustling on their own terms. The material below avoids a "social problems" focus; to some extent, I deliberately reverse that focus. Insofar as I treat of social problems, they are not the problems posed by the hustler but for him; not the difficulties he creates for others, but the difficulties that others create for him as he pursues his career.

This approach "from within" has partly dictated the organization of my materials. Some sections below are built around conceptual categories derived less from sociologists than from hustlers, in the hope that this may help the reader to see hustling more nearly as hustlers see it. The disadvantage for the scientifically-minded reader is that the underlying sociological framework may be obscured. Therefore I wish to point out that this framework is basically that of Everett Hughes's approach to occupational sociology.

I try mainly to answer three types of questions: *(a) The work situation.* How is the hustler's work structured? What skills are required of him? With whom does he interact on the job? What does he want from them, and how does he try to get it? How do they make it easy or hard for him? *(b) Careers.* Who becomes a hustler? How? What job risks or contingencies does the hustler face? When and how? What is the nature of colleagueship in hustling? What are the measures of success and failure in the career? In what ways does aging affect the hustler's job skills or ability to handle other career problems? What leads to retirement? *(c) The external world.* What is the place of the hustler's work situation and career in the larger society? What changes in the structure of that society affect his work situation or career?

PREVIOUS RESEARCH

A bibliographic check reveals no decent research on poolroom hustling, sociological or otherwise. Apart from an occasional work of fiction in which hustling figures, there are merely a few impressionistic accounts in newspapers and popular magazines. With a couple of exceptions, each article is based on interviews with only one or two hustlers. No article analyzes hustling on any but the most superficial level or provides a well-rounded description. The fullest survey of the subject not only omits much that is vital, but contains numerous errors of fact and interpretation.[2]

The desirability of a study of hustling first struck me upon hearing comments by people who saw the movie *The Hustler* (late 1961, re-released spring 1964). Audience members who are not poolroom habitués regard the movie as an accurate por-

[2] Jack Olsen, "The Pool Hustlers," *Sports Illustrated,* Vol. 14 (March 20, 1961), pp. 71–77. Jack Richardson's "The Noblest Hustlers," [*Esquire,* Vol. IX (September, 1963), pp. 94, 96, 98] contains a few worthwhile observations, but it is sketchy, ill-balanced, and suffers much from editorial garbling, all of which makes it both confusing and misleading for the uninitiated. One article conveys quite well the lifestyle of a particular hustler: Dale Shaw, "Anatomy of a Pool Hustler," *Saga: The Magazine for Men,* Vol. 23 (November, 1961), pp. 52–55, 91–93. Useful historical data are in Edward John Vogeler's "The Passing of the Pool Shark," *American Mercury,* Vol. 8 (November, 1939) pp. 346–51. For hustling as viewed within the context of the history of pool in America, see Robert Coughlan's "Pool: Its Players and Its Sharks," *Life,* Vol. 31 (October 8, 1951), pp. 159 ff.; although Coughlan's account of the game's history contains errors and his specific consideration of hustling is brief (p. 166), the latter is accurate.

trait of the contemporary hustling "scene." The movie does indeed truly depict some social characteristics of pool and billiard hustlers and some basic techniques of hustling. But it neglects others of crucial importance. Moreover, the movie scarcely begins to take proper account of the social structure within which hustling techniques are used and which strongly affects their use. *The Hustler* is a reasonably good but highly selective reflection of the poolroom hustling scene as it existed not later than the mid-1930's. And as a guide to today's hustling scene— the terms on which it presents itself and on which the audience takes it—the movie is quite misleading.

METHOD AND SAMPLE

My study of poolroom hustling extended over eight months. It proceeded by a combination of: (a) direct observation of hustlers as they hustled; (b) informal talks, sometimes hours long, with hustlers; (c) participant observation—as hustler's opponent, as hustler's backer, and as hustler. Since methods (b) and (c) drew heavily on my personal involvement with the poolroom world, indeed are inseparable from it, I summarize aspects of that involvement below.

Billiard playing is my chief recreation. I have frequented poolrooms for over 20 years, and at one poolroom game, three-cushion billiards, am considered a far better than average player. In recent years I have played an average of more than six hours per week in various New York poolrooms, and played as much in the poolrooms of Chicago for most of the eight years I lived there. In the course of traveling I have played occasionally in the major rooms of other cities, such as the poolrooms on Market Street in San Francisco, West 25th Street in Cleveland, West Lexington in Baltimore, and the room on 4th and Main in Los Angeles.

My social background is different from that of the overwhelming majority of adult poolroom players. The latter are of lower-class origin. As with many American sports (e.g., base-

ball), pool and billiards are played by teenagers from all classes
but only the players of lower-class background tend to continue
far into adulthood. (And as far as poolroom games are concerned, even at the teenage level the lower class contributes a
disproportionately large share of players.) But such differences
—the fact that I went to college, do highbrow work, etc.—
create no problems of acceptance. In most good-sized poolrooms the adult regulars usually include a few people like myself who are in the poolroom world but not of it. They are
there because they like to play, and are readily accepted because they like to play.

The poolroom I play in most regularly is the principal "action room" in New York and perhaps in the country, the room
in which heavy betting on games occurs most often; sometimes,
particularly after 1:00 A.M., the hustlers in the room well outnumber the non-hustlers. Frequently I play hustlers for money
(nearly always on a handicap basis) and occasionally I hustle
some non-hustlers, undertaking the latter activity primarily to
recoup losses on the former. I have been a backer for two
hustlers.

I know six hustlers well, and during the eight months of the
study I talked or played with over 50 more. All are now usually
based in New York, except for two in Chicago, two in Cleveland, one in Philadelphia, one itinerant hustler whose home base
is Boston and another whose home base is in North Carolina.
However, the hustlers based in New York are of diverse regional origins; almost a third grew up and started their hustling
careers in other states.

It is not possible to demonstrate the representativeness of
this sample because the universe (all U.S. pool and billiard
hustlers) is not known exactly. But the hustlers I asked about
the number of real hustlers in America, i.e., the number of
people whose exclusive or primary occupation is hustling, generally agree that today the number is quite small. In response to
my queries about the total number of poolroom hustlers, one
hustler said "thousands" and another said "there must be a
thousand," but the next highest estimate was "maybe 400" and

somewhat lesser estimates were made by nineteen hustlers. Moreover, the three hustlers making the highest estimates have rarely been out of New York, whereas over half the others either come from other parts of the country or have made several road trips. It seems safe to assume that the sample is at least representative of big-city hustlers. Also, it is probable that it includes the majority of part-time hustlers in New York, and certain that it includes a good majority of the full-time hustlers in New York.

POOLROOM BETTING: THE STRUCTURE OF "ACTION"

Hustling involves betting against one's opponent, by definition. But the converse is not true. The majority of poolroom games on which opponents bet do not involve any element of hustling. In order to understand how hustling enters the picture, one must first establish a perspective that encompasses all betting on poolroom games, hustled or not.

In pool or billiard games, the betting relationship has three possible modes: (1) player bets against player; (2) player against spectator; (3) spectator against spectator. In most games only the first mode occurs, but combinations of the first and second are frequent, and slightly less so are combinations of the first and third. Combinations of all three are uncommon, but do occur when there is more "ready action" offered to the players by the spectators than the players can or wish to absorb. I have never seen the second mode occur alone, nor a combination of second and third. I have seen the third mode occur alone only twice—at professional tournaments. The betting relationship, then, involves the mode player-vs.-player, whatever additional modes there may be.

If two mediocre players are betting, say, upward of $15 per game, and at another table two excellent players are playing for only a token amount, the first table will invariably draw many more people around it. The great majority of spectators,

whether or not they bet much and whatever their own degree
of playing skill, are attracted more by the size of the action than
the quality of the performance. (A visiting Danish billiardist
tells me this is not so in Europe, and also that betting on poolroom games is far less frequent there than in America.)

There is an old American poolroom tradition that players
should make some kind of bet with each other, if only a small
one. This tradition remains strong in every public poolroom I
know. (It is weak in the pool or billiard rooms of private men's
clubs and YMCAs, weaker still in student unions, and virtually
nonexistent in faculty clubs.) When one player says to another,
"Let's just play sociable," as often as not he means that they
should play for only a dollar or two, and at the very least means
that they should play "for the time" (the loser paying the
check). It is only some of the newer and least skilled players
who refuse to bet at all (who want to "split the time"), and
nearly always they rapidly become socialized to the betting
tradition by a carrot-and-stick process—the stick being that it
is often hard to get a game otherwise, the carrot that better
players are always willing to give poorer ones a handicap (a
"spot"). Most of the regular players will not even play for the
check only, but insist on a little money changing hands "just to
make the game interesting." The player who claims that just
playing the game is interesting enough in itself is regarded as
something of a freak.

Few serious bettors, hustlers excepted, care for big action;
but nearly all, including hustlers, want fast action. Although
they may not want to bet much per game, they want the cash
to change hands fairly quickly. Consequently, in an action room
the standard games are redesigned for this purpose. Some are
simply shortened: players gambling at snooker will remove all
the red balls but one; or three-cushion billiard players will play
games of 15, 20, or 25 points instead of the usual 30, 40, or
50. In straight pool (pocket billiards), where the standard game
is 125 or 150 points, good players are usually reluctant to play
a much shorter game because scoring is so easy—any good

player can occasionally run more than 50 balls—that shortening the game makes it too much a matter of chance. Therefore, in an action room one finds most of the pool players playing some variant of the game that not only requires high skill but also minimizes chance, and that therefore can be short (taking only 5 to 20 minutes per game). Today the chief of these variants are "nine ball" and "one pocket" (also called "pocket apiece"), although there are several others, such as "eight ball," "bank pool," and "rotation."

Every poolroom has at least one "No Gambling" sign on display, but no poolroom enforces it. The sign is merely a formal gesture for the eyes of the law (and in some cities required by law). It is enforced only in that the proprietor sometimes may ask players to keep payoffs out of sight—not to toss the money on the table after the game—if the room is currently "heaty," e.g., if an arrest has recently been made there. Police are hardly ever concerned to stop the gambling on poolroom games, and everyone knows it. (But police sometimes check to see that the minimum age law is observed, so proprietors will often ask youths for identification.) Betting is so taken for granted that in most poolrooms the proprietor—the very man who displays a "No Gambling" sign over his desk—will on request hold the players' stake money.

However, in no poolroom does the house take a cut of the action; the proprietor gets no fee for permitting gambling or holding stake money, and wouldn't dream of asking for one. His payment from bettors is simply that they comprise most of his custom in equipment rental. And hustlers, as he and they well know, count in this regard far beyond their numbers, for they play much oftener and longer than other customers; indeed, they virtually live in the poolroom.

The only non-bettor whose payment is somewhat related to the size of the action is the rack boy (if one is used), the person who racks up the balls for the players after each frame. The bigger the action, the larger the tip he can expect, and if one player comes out very much ahead he tips the rack boy lavishly.

The rack boy's position is thus analogous to that of the golf caddie, except that a rack boy is used in only about half of hustler-vs.-hustler contests and in but a tiny fraction of other contests. Sometimes he is an employee (sweeper, etc.) of the poolroom, but more often he is a spectator performing as rack boy on an *ad hoc* basis.

NON-HUSTLED POOLROOM GAMBLING

Hustling is *not* involved when the games played for money are any of the following:

(a) *Non-hustler vs. non-hustler*. A "sociable" game in which the bet is a token one. The only betting is player vs. player.

(b) *Non-hustler vs. non-hustler*. A game for significantly more than a token amount. The players play even-up if they are fairly equal. If they are aware of a significant difference in skill levels, the weaker player is given an appropriate handicap. Usually the betting is just between players; rarely, one or both players will bet spectators; spectators do not bet each other.

(c) *Hustler vs. non-hustler*. The players are aware of the difference in skills, and this is properly taken into account via an appropriate spot. Usually the betting is only player vs. player, though sometimes spectators bet players or each other. The hustler tries to avoid this type of game, and agrees to it only when he has nothing better to do.

(d) *Hustler vs. hustler*. Each player knows the other's mettle, if only by reputation ("Minnesota Fats" vs. "Fast Eddy" in *The Hustler,* for example). The hustler, contrary to the impression given by the movie, does *not* prefer this type of game (though he does prefer it to the foregoing type) and does *not* regard it as hustling. But he plays it often because he often can't get the kind of game he wants (a true "hustle") and this alternative does offer him excitement—not only the greatest challenge to his playing skill, but the most action. The average bet between two hustlers is much higher than in any other type of poolroom contest.[3] And betting modes 2 and 3 (player vs. spectator, spectator vs. spectator) occur much more often.

Be that as it may, the hustler much prefers to hustle, which means to be in a game set up so as to be pretty much a sure thing for him, a game that "you're not allowed to lose" as the hustler puts it. In order to achieve this, to truly hustle, he engages in deception. The centrality of deception in pool or billiard hustling is perhaps best indicated by the fact that the poolroom hustlers' argot originated that widespread American slang dictum, "never give a sucker an even break." [4]

THE HUSTLER'S METHODS OF DECEPTION

The structure of a gambling game determines what methods of deception, if any, may be used in it. In many games (dice, cards, etc.) one can deceive one's opponent by various techniques of cheating. Pool and billiard games are so structured that this method is virtually impossible. (Once in a great while,

[3] When two high-betting hustlers agree to play each other there is often a real race among poorer spectators to offer rack-boy services because, as previously noted, if one is engaged for such a session he can expect a good tip. I witnessed one six-hour session between hustlers in which the winning hustler came out $800 ahead and tipped the rack boy $50.

[4] Its pool-hustler origin is noted by Vogeler, *op. cit.*, p. 347. It is recorded in none of the slang sourcebooks (Mencken, Mathews, Berrey and Van den Bark, *et al.*) except Harold Wentworth and Stuart Berg Flexner, *Dictionary of American Slang* (New York: T. Y. Crowell, 1960), p. 527. Wentworth and Flexner do not attempt to account for the phrase's origin. They claim that it dates to around 1835, but this seems impossibly early. The only source they cite is its use as the title of a 1941 W. C. Fields movie.

Actually, Fields used the phrase earlier in his *Poppy* (1936), where it is his exit line and the last line of the movie. Fields's partiality to "never give a sucker an even break" is thoroughly in keeping with Vogeler's account of the origin of the phrase: Fields was the son of a Philadelphia poolroom owner, spent much of his boyhood in his father's poolroom, was an excellent player, and built his funniest vaudeville act around his pool-playing skill (at the act's climax he sank fifteen balls with one shot). Cf. Douglas Gilbert, *American Vaudeville* (New York: Whittlesey House, 1940), pp. 273–74.

against a particularly unalert opponent, one can surreptitiously add a point or two to one's score—but such opportunity is rare, usually involves risk of discovery that is judged to be too great, and seldom means the difference between winning and losing anyway; so no player counts on it.) One's every move and play is completely visible, easily watched by one's opponent and by spectators; nor is it possible to achieve anything via previous tampering with the equipment.

However, one structural feature of pool or billiards readily lends itself to deceit: on each shot, the difference between success and failure is a matter of a small fraction of an inch. In pool or billiards it is peculiarly easy, even for the average player, to miss one's shot deliberately and still look good (unlike, say, nearly all card games, where if one does not play one's cards correctly this is soon apparent). On all shots except the easiest ones, it is impossible to tell if a player is deliberately not trying his best.

The hustler exploits this fact so as to deceive his opponent as to his (the hustler's) true level of skill (true "speed"). It is so easily exploited that, when playing good opponents, usually the better hustlers even disdain it, pocket nearly every shot they have (intentionally miss only some very difficult shots), and rely chiefly on related but subtler techniques of failure beyond the remotest suspicion of most players. For example, such a hustler may strike his cue ball hard and with too much spin ("english"), so that the spin is transferred to the object ball and the object ball goes into the pocket but jumps out again; or he may scratch (losing a point and his turn), either by "accidentally" caroming his cue ball into a pocket or by hitting his cue ball hard and with too much top-spin so that it jumps off the table; or, most commonly, he pockets his shot but, by striking his cue ball just a wee bit too hard or too softly or with too much or too little english, he leaves himself "safe" (ends up with his cue ball out of position, so that he hasn't another shot). In such wise the hustler feigns less competence than he has.

Hustling, then, involves not merely the ability to play well, but the use of a kind of "short con." Sometimes the hustler doesn't need to employ any con to get his opponent to the table, sometimes he does; but he always employs it in attempting to keep his opponent there.

The best hustler is not necessarily the best player among the hustlers. He has to be a very good player, true, but beyond a certain point his playing ability is not nearly so important as his skill at various kinds of conning. Also, he has to possess personality traits that make him "rocklike," able to exploit fully his various skills—playing, conning, others—in the face of assorted pressures and temptations not to exploit them fully.

THE HUSTLER'S CARDINAL RULE

As the foregoing indicates, the hustler's cardinal rule is: *don't show your real speed.* Of course, an exception is permitted if by some miracle the hustler finds himself hustled, finds himself in a game with someone he thought would be easy but who turns out to be tough. But this is not supposed to happen, and it rarely does. For one thing, hustlers generally know each other, or of each other, and their respective skill levels. Secondly, any pool or billiard game is overwhelmingly a game of skill rather than luck—even in the chanciest type of poolroom game the element of skill counts for much more than in any card game whatsoever—and this means it is possible to rate the skill levels of various players (to "handicap" them) along small gradations with a high degree of accuracy. For example, if one has seen the three-cushion billiard players X and Y play various people over a period of time, it is possible to arrive at the judgment "On a 30-point game, X is two or three points better than Y" and to be dead right about it in at least eight out of ten contests between them.

The corollaries of the hustler's chief rule are: (a) The hustler must restrain himself from making many of the extremely difficult shots. Such restraint is not easy, because the thrill of making a fancy shot that brings applause from the audience is hard to resist. But the hustler must resist, or else it would make less believable his misses on more ordinary shots. (b) He must play so that the games he wins are won by only a small margin. (c) He must let his opponent win an occasional game.

It may be thought that once a hustler has engaged an opponent, a bet has been agreed upon and the stake money put up, and the game has started, the hustler might safely let out all the stops. This would be terribly short-sighted.

In the first place, as noted earlier, the typical non-hustler bets only a small amount on the game. The hustler's only hope of making real money, therefore, is to extend the first game into a series of games, entice his opponent into doubling up when he is behind, etc. If the hustler does this well, the opponent will hang on for a long time, may even come back after the first session to play him on another day, turn into a real "fish" (the poolroom term for an inferior opponent who doesn't catch on that he's outclassed, and keeps coming back for more). And when the opponent starts demanding a spot, as sooner or later he will, the hustler can offer him his (the hustler's) average winning margin, or even a little better, and still have a safe game.

Secondly, there are spectators to take into account. Some of them will bet the hustler if he offers the non-hustler a seemingly fair spot. More importantly, some of them are potential opponents. Nearly all poolroom spectators are also players. The hustler doesn't want to look too good to spectators either.

He knows that as he beats various opponents his reputation will rise, and that increasingly he'll have to offer spots to people, but he wants to keep his reputation as low as possible as long as possible with as many people as possible. He also knows that he has to play superbly on occasion—that he will play fellow hustlers when there's no other action around, and that then he must show more skill—but he wants to keep these occasions few. (It helps considerably, by the way, that because hustler-vs.-hustler games occur when hustlers give up hope of

finding other action, these games usually take place after mid-
night when there aren't so many non-hustler potential victims
around to watch.)

The sooner everyone in the poolroom knows the hustler's
true speed, the sooner he exhausts the real hustling possibilities
among the room's regular players. Such a situation constitutes
one of the career crises that every hustler has to face. (For
reasons which will become apparent below, he now has to face
it earlier in his career than hustlers formerly did.) When it
occurs, either he must move on to a room where he's less
known or, if he stays in the room, he has to take games he
shouldn't take or else restrict his pickings to strangers who wan-
der in.

Job-Related Skills and Traits

Although the hallmarks of the good hustler are playing skill
and the temperamental ability to consistently look poorer than
he is, there are other skills and traits that aid him in hustling.
Some are related to deceiving his opponent, some not.

Chief of these is argumentative skill in arranging the terms
of the match, the ability to "make a game." The prospective
opponent, if he has seen the hustler play, may when approached
claim that the hustler is too good for him or ask for too high a
spot, i.e., one that is fair or even better. The hustler, like the
salesman, is supposed to be familiar with standard objections
and "propositions" for overcoming them.

Another side of the ability to make a game reveals itself
when the prospective opponent simply can't be argued out of
demanding a spot that is unfair to the hustler, or can be convinced to play only if the hustler offers such a spot. At that
point the hustler should of course refuse to play. There is often
a temptation to do otherwise, not only because the hustler is
proud of his skill but because action is his lifeblood (which is
why he plays other hustlers when he can't find a hustle), and
there may be no other action around. He must resist the tempta-

tion. In the good hustler's view, no matter how badly you want action, it is better not to play at all than to play when you are disadvantaged; otherwise you are just hustling yourself. (But the hustler often will, albeit with much argument and the greatest reluctance, agree to give a fair spot if that's the only way he can get action.)

The hustler, when faced, as he very often is, with an opponent who knows him as such, of course finds that his ability to make a game assumes greater importance than his ability to feign lack of skill. In such situations, indeed, his game-making ability is just as important as his actual playing ability.

On the other hand, the hustler must have "heart" (courage). The *sine qua non* is that he is a good "money player," can play his best when heavy action is riding on the game (as many non-hustlers can't). Also, he is not supposed to let a bad break or distractions in the audience upset him. (He may pretend to get rattled on such occasions, but that's just part of his con.) Nor should the quality of his game deteriorate when, whether by miscalculation on his part or otherwise, he finds himself much further behind than he would like to be. Finally, if it is necessary to get action, he should not be afraid to tackle an opponent whom he knows to be just about as good as he is.

A trait often working for the hustler is stamina. As a result of thousands of hours of play, all the right muscles are toughened up. He is used to playing many hours at a time, certainly much more used to it than the non-hustler is. This is valuable because sometimes, if the hustler works it right, he can make his opponent forget about quitting for such a "silly" reason as being tired, can extend their session through the night and into the next day. In such sessions it is most often in the last couple of hours, when the betting per game is usually highest, that the hustler makes his biggest killing.

Additional short-con techniques are sometimes used. One hustler, for example, entices opponents by the ancient device of pretending to be sloppy-drunk. Other techniques show more imagination. For example, a hustler preparing for a road trip mentioned to me that before leaving town he was going to buy a soldier's uniform: "I walk into a strange room in uniform and I've got it made. Everybody likes to grab a soldier."

Finally, the hustler—the superior hustler at any rate—has enough flexibility and good sense to break the "rules" when the occasion demands it, will modify standard techniques when he encounters non-standard situations. An example: Once I entered a poolroom just as a hustler I know, X, was finishing a game with non-hustler Y. X beat Y soundly, by a higher margin than a hustler should beat anyone, and at that for only $3. Y went to the bathroom, whereupon I admonished X, "What's the matter with you? You know you're not allowed to win that big." X replied:

> Yeah, sure, but you see that motherfucking S over there? [nodding discreetly in the direction of one of the spectators]. Well, about an hour ago when I came in he and Y were talking, and when S saw me he whispered something to Y. So I had a hunch he was giving him the wire [tipping him off] that I was pretty good. And then in his middle game it looked like Y was stalling a little [missing deliberately] to see what I would do, so then I was sure he got the wire on me. I had to beat him big so he'll think he knows my top speed. But naturally I didn't beat him as big as I *could* beat him. Now he'll come back cryin' for a spot and bigger action, and I'll nail him.

And he did nail him.[5]

THE ART OF DUMPING

As we saw, the structure of a pool or billiard game makes it virtually impossible for the hustler to cheat his opponent. By "stalling" (deliberately missing some shots, leaving himself out

---

[5] This sort of situation is unusual. One part of the poolroom code, adhered to by nearly all regular players, holds that a player is supposed to watch out for himself in the matches he gets into, find out for himself whom he can and cannot beat. Ordinarily one does not warn a player about who is superior or who the hustlers are, unless one is a close friend of that player. (And even if one is a friend, the code demands that such a warning be given only before any match is in prospect; that is, once a player has started to "make a game" with another, third parties are supposed to stay out.)

of position, etc.) and by "lemoning" or "lemonading" an occasional game in the session (winning in a deliberately sloppy and seemingly lucky manner, or deliberately losing the game), the hustler keeps his opponent on the hook and entices him into heavier action, but such deception falls short of outright cheating. However, in examining betting we saw that there is considerable variation in the interpersonal superstructure of the game, i.e., that there are several types of betting relationships between and among players and spectators. One of these varieties does lead to outright cheating by the hustler—not cheating his opponent, but cheating some spectators.

When two hustlers play each other, not only is the betting between players relatively heavy, but the betting of spectators against players is also, typically, at its height. Therefore, two hustlers sometimes will agree before their session that if, on any game, there is a good disparity between the amounts of action that each gets from spectators, the player with the most to gain from side bets with spectators will win the game and the players will later share the profits. The amount that spectators bet each other is of course irrelevant to such calculations, and in such circumstances the amount that the players bet each other automatically becomes a phony bet, strictly for deluding the spectators.

For example, one such game I know of went as follows: Hustler A played hustler B for $70. A's side bets with spectators totaled $100 and B's side bets with spectators totaled $380. Therefore A deliberately lost to B, paying him $70 and paying $100 to spectators, with B collecting $70 from A and $380 from spectators. Later, in private, B gave A $310 (the $70 that A had "lost" to B, the $100 that A had paid to the audience, plus $140 or one-half the overall amount won from the audience). Each player thus made $140 on the deal.

Sometimes the hustlers will set up the audience for such disparity in side betting, via previous games in the session. An example: Hustler X played hustler Y for $20 per game. By pre-arrangement, both players refused to make side bets with spectators on the first three games and player Y deliberately

lost the first three games. At the end of the third game Y became enraged, claiming that bad breaks had beat him, that X
was just lucky, etc.; he raised his bet with X to $50 and also
offered to bet spectators. Naturally, he got lots of action from
spectators—and just as naturally he won the fourth game.

More commonly, however, such setting up does not occur.
Rather, the hustlers will agree before their session that they will
play each other in earnest and the bets between them will be
real, but that if there is a disparity in side betting with spectators on a given game and one player gives the other a prear-
ranged signal (gives him "the office," as the hustler's argot has
it), the player with the most side action will win.

In the hustler's argot, the above type of deliberate losing is
called "dumping." It is always distinguished from "lemoning"
(where deliberate losing is strictly a means of conning one's
opponent). Though all hustlers use the verb "to dump" in referring to a game that the hustler deliberately loses for the
purpose of cheating spectators, hustlers vary in the object they
attach to the verb. Some hustlers would say that the hustler
who lost "dumped the game," others that he "dumped to" his
opponent, and others that he (or both players in collaboration)
"dumped the bettors." Some hustlers on occasion prefer a nom-
inal use: "the game was a dump."

Because dumping involves outright cheating and could lead
to serious, in fact violent, reprisals if discovered, it is the aspect
of hustling that hustlers are most evasive about. No hustler likes
to own up to dumping, even in talk with other hustlers. One
learns about dumping indirectly, via hustlers' comments on
other hustlers, and only rarely via a hustler's direct admission
that he has engaged in it. It is my impression that such reti-
cence is always pragmatic rather than moral, i.e., that no hustler
has strong compunctions about dumping and that every long-
time hustler has dumped at least on occasion.

Although dumping is a possibility whenever two hustlers
playing each other make unequal amounts of side bets with
spectators, it actually occurs in only a minority of such situa-

tions.[6] For dumping is risky even when it is not literally discovered; sometimes the spectators' suspicions are aroused even though nothing can be proven, and hustlers can't afford to have this happen often, because it would kill their chances of side betting.

In this regard there are two kinds of spectator-bettors that the hustler distinguishes and takes account of: First, there are the ignorant majority of spectators who don't know about dumping; the hustler doesn't want talk, much less actual knowledge, of dumping to reach their ears. Second—and equally important to the hustler because, though they are in the minority, they bet more—there are some knowledgeable spectators (including other hustlers) who know about dumping but *also* know that it occurs in only a minority of hustler-vs.-hustler contests and therefore will often risk a bet. That is to say, just as some horse players assume that at certain tracks there probably will be one race per day that is fixed (one race "for the boys") and are willing to discount this because it's only one race out of eight or nine, similarly there are poolroom spectators who will bet on one hustler against another because they know that dumping occurs but seldom. (Among the knowledgeable spectators there are also, of course, some cautious types who refuse to make such bets because of a possible dump, even though they know the odds are against it.)

In sum, the fact that spectators will bet players in hustler-vs.-hustler games not only permits dumping but at the same time restrains its extent. Hustlers must severely limit their dumping, both to prevent it becoming known to the ignorant and, just as importantly, to prevent knowledgeable spectators from feeling that hustlers *generally* dump when they play each other. No hustler wants to get a reputation as a dumper; therefore he cautiously picks his spots. As a result, dumping provides only a small portion of his true hustling income, i.e., his

[6] Under certain special circumstances, dumping can also occur when there are no bets with spectators or such bets are approximately equal on both sides; see below.

"sure-thing" income. The great bulk of such income derives from his games with non-hustler opponents.

THE HUSTLER AND HIS BACKER

The hustler frequently uses a backer, who pays the losses if the hustler loses and receives 50 per cent of any winnings. A backer hardly ever assumes any managerial function. All he does is put up the hustler's stake money in return for a half share in the profits.

Once in a very great while, a hustler will work out a standing agreement for backing, i.e., have someone agree to back him regularly. There is no time limit specified for such an arrangement; the deal lasts only as long as both parties consent to it.

But almost always the hustler has no standing agreement with a backer. Rather, he looks for backing on an *ad hoc* basis as the occasion for backing arises. The "occasion" is not that the hustler decides, in the abstract, to play on someone else's risk capital; it is a specific match with a particular opponent, whose handicap terms (if any) the hustler has already arranged or knows he can get. Indeed, even a top-notch hustler rarely can get backing without being able to tell the backer who the prospective opponent is and what the terms of the game are; the hustler has to convince the backer that the particular deal is a good one.

After tentatively arranging a game with his opponent, the hustler asks one of his acquaintances in the room to back him, and if he can't find backing in the room he phones a potential backer to hurry on down with some cash. Sometimes the hustler enters the poolroom with his backer in tow.

The backer specifies the maximum amount per game that he is willing to invest, but makes no guarantee about a total investment. That is, if the hustler starts to lose, the backer can pull out after any game. And if the hustler starts winning, he cannot then bet only his "own" money and dispense with the backer; the backer is in for 50 per cent of the profit made on the entire session.

Under what conditions does the hustler seek a backer? The obvious answer is that when the hustler is broke or nearly broke (as he very often is), he looks for backing, and when he has his own money to invest he plays with that. This is indeed how the average hustler operates. The superior hustler, however, figures more angles. As one of the most intelligent hustlers explained to me:

> If you've got lockup action [a game impossible to lose] and you're broke or maybe you need a bigger stake, you should first try like hell to *borrow* the dough. It's crazy to cut somebody in on action like that unless you have to. The other big thing—what some of these jerks don't understand—is that when you have a real tough game you should *always* look for a backer, even if you've got the dough. You should take out insurance.

The backer, then, should not assume he is being approached for backing because the hustler can raise stake money no other way (though this is usually the case), but has to consider the possibility that it's because the hustler has a very difficult game he wants to "insure."

Also, the backer must consider the possibility that he may be dumped by the hustler: If the hustler is playing a colleague, they may have agreed that one of them will win the good majority of games and that they will later split the profits. (When both hustlers making such an agreement are using backers, the decision as to which hustler will lose is more or less arbitrary. If one hustler is using a backer and the other is not, it is of course the former who agrees to lose.) Or, if the hustler is playing a non-hustler with whom no such collusion is possible, he may deliberately lose on the backer's money until the backer quits, and then, after the backer has left the room or on some other occasion, the hustler, playing with his own money, will slaughter the opponent he has set up on the backer's money.

All in all, it takes as much sophistication to be a good backer as to be a good hustler.

The Hustler as Con Man

As several parts of this study illustrate in detail, hustling demands a continuous and complicated concern with how one is seen by others. Attention to this matter is an ineluctably pervasive requirement of the hustler's trade, and is beset with risks and contradictions. The hustler has not only the concerns that one ordinarily has about being esteemed for one's skills, but develops, in addition to and partly in conflict with such concerns, a complex set of special needs or desires about how others should evaluate him, reactions to their evaluations, and behaviors designed to manipulate such evaluating.

The hustler is a certain kind of con man. And conning, by definition, involves extraordinary manipulation of other people's impressions of reality and especially of one's self, creating "false impressions." [7] If one compares the hustler with the more usual sorts of con men described by David Maurer in *The Big Con,* part of the hustler's specialness is seen to lie in this: the structural contexts within which he operates—the game, the setting of the game within the poolroom, the setting of the poolroom within the larger social structure—are not only more predetermined but more constraining. Structures do not "work for" the poolroom hustler to anywhere near the extent that they often do for other con men, and hence he must involve himself in more personal ways with active, continuous conning.

The point is not simply that the hustler can't find an ideal structural context, but that much less than the ordinary con man is he able to bend a structure toward the ideal or create one *ab ovo* (come up with an analogue of the con man's

[7] Of course, conning is only a matter of degree, in that all of us are concerned in many ways to manipulate others' impressions of us, and so one can, if one wishes, take the view that every man is at bottom a con man. This form of "disenchantment of the world" is central to Herman Melville's *The Confidence Man* (one of the bitterest novels in all of American literature) and to the sociological writings of Erving Goffman. Its principal corollary is the view expressed by hustlers, by other career criminals, and by Thorstein Veblen, that all businessmen are thieves.

"store"). That is, the hustler is far less able to be a "producer" or "director" of ideal social "scenes." To a much greater extent he must work in poor settings, and to a correspondingly greater extent he must depend on being a continuously self-aware "actor." [8] (In this connection, note the ease with which many passages of this essay could be restated in dramaturgical or Goffmaniacal terms.)

There is another significant respect in which the hustler's conning differs structurally from the work of ordinary con men. The latter's work, according to Maurer, falls into one or the other of two structurally distinct types of con games: the short con, in which the mark is played for the money he happens to be carrying, or else the big con, in which an essential feature is that the mark is "put on the send" to withdraw much larger sums from his bank. (Some con men also on occasion "throw the send into" a short-con game, but this is unusual.) There is no analogous distinction made by pool hustlers in theory or practice. Virtually every hustle is in Maurer's sense a short con, i.e., the sucker is simply taken for the cash he has on him at the time, or as much of it as he will allow himself to lose.

There are two situations in which the hustler's conning involves his victim going on the send, but they are accidental and rare; the hustler doesn't expect them, though he is of course pleased when one or the other of them happens: (a) As we have noted, the ideal kind of sucker is the "fish" who doesn't realize he can never win and makes himself available on other days for return matches, much like the sort of mark whom con

---

[8] The kinds of structural problems faced today by the pool or billiard hustler are by no means all endemic; some are the result of recent social change (see pp. 76–78 below). On the other hand, such change has not created structural problems for all types of hustling. Today the golf hustler, for example, finds that with precious little "acting" he can (a) get heavy action from non-hustlers, (b) lose the majority of the eighteen holes and still clean up, and at the same time (c) not be suspected as a hustler. The structure of the game of golf itself, the peculiar structurally predetermined variations in the betting relationship as one makes the round of the course ("presses," etc.), and the present setting of the game within the larger society—all these combine to create a situation that is tailor-made for hustling. But that is another story.

men call an "addict." In order to reinforce any propensity his
victim might have for being or becoming a fish, the hustler tries
to win the last game of a match by only a small margin even
though he *knows* it is the last game, i.e., knows that after he
beats the sucker the latter will quit because he is cleaned out
or unwilling to risk the small amount he may have left. On very
rare occasion, to the hustler's surprise and delight, when the
sucker is thus cleaned out he may not end the match but instead become a sort of instant fish (my term, not used by
hustlers): he may have the hustler wait while he (the sucker)
runs out to get more cash and comes back with same. (b) As a
result of having watched the hustler stall with some other opponent (or in solitary practice), the sucker may decide that before
he challenges the hustler, or accepts the hustler's challenge, he
should go get more of a bankroll so he can make bigger bets.

Although in both of the above situations the victim goes on
the send as a result of the hustler's actions, such actions are
not, strictly speaking, calculated to achieve that result. The
sucker essentially puts himself on the send.

The hustler needs to be continually concerned about evaluation of him by other persons. But the nature and degree of his
concern vary with the particular kind of "others" that these
persons represent. The victim or prospective victim, the hustler's
orientation toward whom we have discussed at several points, is
only one kind of other. Obviously the hustler must take cogni-
zance of at least two additional types of significant others: outsiders and colleagues. Let us look at how he relates to them.

OUTSIDERS

By "outsiders" I do not mean those poolroom players and
spectators who aren't hustlers (most such people most of the
time are considered by the hustler to be prospective victims),
but rather the public at large whose interests lie outside the
poolroom world entirely. As far as the hustler is concerned, the

central fact about such people is that they are not potential sources of income for him.

Another relevant fact about such people was noted at the beginning of this essay: nearly all of them, insofar as they have any knowledge or opinion about hustling at all, stigmatize the hustler and his trade. But this fact—and here hustlers differ in a major way from other socially deviant groups—is not at all important in hustler thinking. The fact that hustlers are put down by society at large is extraordinarily rare as a topic of hustlers' conversation or consciousness. Nor, despite the fact that hustlers come from a subculture whose values differ from those on the basis of which they are stigmatized, do they bother to develop a definite counter-ideology about why outsiders should themselves be put down. In this respect hustlers seem to be unlike, say, most drug users, homosexuals, bohemians and jazz musicians, and unlike the great majority of career criminals.

To be sure, the hustler is aware that outsiders in general stigmatize him. But he is aware of it less often, and less strongly, than other people are aware of their negative status in the larger society—for he comes in contact with it far less. The homosexual may elicit negative reactions in a variety of "straight" work situations and other public situations unless he is successful in disguising his homosexuality (and even then he hears a lot of putdowns of "queers"); the Negro, even if he elects to live in the heart of his ghetto and remain as "black" as possible, is raised on white mass media and at the least cannot help internalizing white ideals of physical attractiveness (on this see Chapter 4); the typical criminal cannot pick up a newspaper or look at TV without being faced with the fact that the public rejects him and his kind. The hustler's lifespace and lifeways, however, cut him off much more fully from outsiders' negative judgments. Unlike Negroes, he is segregated not only from his "betters" but from their opinions of him. There are three reasons for this.

(1) My statement earlier that hustlers "virtually live in the poolroom" was meant literally. About four-fifths of the hustlers

are unmarried. Moreover, almost every unmarried hustler re-
sides by himself in one small furnished room or hotel room,
hardly conducive to developing a "home life." His real psychological home is the job site, the poolroom. This is where he
spends almost all his waking hours. This is not only where he
works but where he loafs, plays, and as often as not eats—
and also where he sleeps when he can't make room rent. In
fine, it is his leisure-place as much as his work-place.

The typical hustler has very few interests outside the poolroom and reads nothing except (sporadically) the racing page
of the newspaper. Even his few outside interests are intermit-
tent: watching sports events on TV once or twice a week,
occasionally making a pickup in a bar and getting laid, once
in a while seeing a movie, going to the track several times a
year, now and then playing cards—that's the sum total of non-
poolroom life for most hustlers.

(2) When the hustler does temporarily take a non-hustling
job, it tends to be one that takes him out of the poolroom
not at all or hardly at all, or else provides only fleeting, frag-
mented contacts with the non-poolroom world.

(3) The hustler seldom runs into non-hustler players who
put him down. First of all, most non-hustler poolroom habitués
not only accept the poolroom tradition that all players should
bet, but tend in varying degrees to accept the "sporting life"
ethic accompanying it (especially the notion that if a player
overmatches himself that's his own problem), and their attitudes toward hustlers range from ignorance or indifference to
tolerance to sympathy to outright admiration. Certainly such
attitudes (except for ignorance) are true of nearly all those
non-hustlers who play regularly in "action rooms."

As for the players who object to hustlers: whether they
play regularly or infrequently, they seldom are in the action
rooms where hustlers hang out but prefer the sedater poolrooms (or, if upper class, prefer to play in private clubs). Also,
more often than not such players are so unperceptive of all
but the crudest hustling that they can't tell a hustler when they

see one. Many a player who believes he has never played a hustler has in fact been hustled by several.

Of course, the hustler doesn't proclaim his trade to the outside world, for typically he has neither a masochistic urge to be put down nor the reactive hostility to majority opinion that one finds in the flamboyant homosexual or "professional Negro" or "professional Jew" and the like. On the other hand, he isn't much concerned with hiding his trade from outsiders so long as openness would not adversely affect his income. He actually runs into putdowns so seldom and his world is so self-contained that the majority's negative opinion neither significantly affects his life-chances nor bruises his psyche.

In other words, though the hustler cares about what the outside world thinks of his role, he cares about it much less than other deviants do. Outsiders as a class may comprise a significant other for the hustler, but they are not a genuine "reference group" for him: he has not even the most latent of aspirations to membership in their world, and thus is not about to change his behavior to accord with their moral standards. As a result he is likely to practice a peculiar kind of inconsistency about revealing his occupation to outsiders— an inconsistency that has the mark not of "conflict" or "ambivalence" but rather of genuine flexibility and free choice, i.e., choice based on rational calculation of what, in any given situation with outsiders, might be most to his advantage.

An example of this flexibility or rational inconsistency in the presence of outsiders may be seen by comparing two samples from the behavior of the man known among hustlers as Wimpy, America's foremost nine-ball hustler, and known to larger circles as a professional player under his real name, Luther Lassiter (on the relation between hustling and professional playing, see below). In April, 1963, he won the World Pocket Billiard Tournament. One day during the tournament— after he had won a game that made it almost certain he would be the next champion—a few spectators, including myself, were talking with him when a reporter from the Associated

Press came up and started interviewing him. The reporter asked, among other things, how Mr. Lassiter made his living— and did he make it playing pool? Wimpy smiled and said no; he said that he lived with his mother, that he had a rich brother who helped him out, and that it just seemed that the good Lord looked after him. Yet only a few weeks later he appeared on a nationwide TV program called *To Tell the Truth,* in which the panelists were to guess which one of three persons, including Lassiter, was a pool hustler, and in which his occupation was revealed. In the first situation, there was nothing to be gained from revealing his occupation to the reporter, and possibly negative consequences for the "image" of pocket billiards—which both the players and the sponsors of the tournament were concerned to improve.[9] In the second situation, there was a nice fee for him in going on TV to own up publicly to his trade.

COLLEAGUESHIP

Colleagueship among hustlers is partly typical of colleagueship in occupations generally, and partly not. One way in which it is untypical has to do with entry to and expulsion from the occupation.

In most kinds of work, the colleague group can debar someone from entry, either by formal means (e.g., deny him job training, or a license, or tools, or union membership) or by informal means (e.g., ostracize him socially, refuse to work with him, deny him the recommendations needed to get work).

[9] Apropos of the public relations or "image-making" aspect of this tournament: members of its sponsoring group, the Billiard Room Proprietors Association of America, admitted to me that because of their desire not to jeopardize the game's comeback attempt (this was the first world tournament held in several years), they had not invited two players who doubtless were superior to at least one of the ten contestants invited. The two uninvited players might have damaged the "image" that the tournament was trying to convey: one of them had recently been in jail on a felony charge, and the other was noted for, among other things, his refusal to wear a tie and the unrelieved profanity of his speech.

But entry to hustling does not involve elements that can be effectively controlled by colleagues. There are no formal entrance criteria such as examinations or licenses or diplomas. And job training (the development of playing and conning ability) is publicly available to anyone, as are the tools of the trade (playing equipment), a workplace (the poolroom), and the market for one's skill (suckers). In most of his job activities, and in all that are truly essential, each hustler is basically an individual entrepreneur. For this reason also, the colleague group cannot really "expel" anyone from hustling.

It is true enough that to enjoy colleagueship means first of all to be recognized and accepted as a colleague by others. But it does not always follow that to be denied colleagueship is to be denied work. It may make the work situation tougher, but by no means impossible. Thus, if a hustler is denied acceptance by other hustlers, it can rule out dumping and other forms of cooperation between him and them, but it has no discernible effect on his main job activity, which is to lure suckers into games with him.

In any case, outright rejection of a hustler by his colleagues, by refusal to cooperate or associate with him, is actually quite rare. It is invoked only on those whose personalities can cause associates plenty of grief. An example: after this study was under way for three months I began avoiding games with one of the hustlers I had until then played billiards with—this on the advice of other hustlers, who warned me that my playing companion was both armed and unpredictably short-tempered.

A colleague group creates *esprit de corps,* a feeling of "we-ness." It also creates awareness that although colleagues are equals, some colleagues are more equal than others; i.e., it creates an intra-occupational stratification system, mostly along the dimension of prestige. I mention these together because in the hustling world the two are peculiarly intertwined: Non-rigged games between hustlers—ever more frequent these days, for reasons to be indicated later—constitute on the one hand intense, focused interaction between friendly colleagues, in the context of an audience consisting largely or exclusively of other colleagues, and thus such games contribute much to group identity feelings. But on the other hand, they are also serious, fierce competitions, whose results provide colleagues with their chief basis for rating a hustler's playing skill, which rating is in turn a major ingredient of his general prestige rank. Thus the *esprit de corps* of the hustling world and its internal stratification system are to some degree functions of each other. That noted, we can now look at each separately.

At the bottom of the prestige hierarchy are those few players with so little skill that, even though they hustle, colleagues question their right to be regarded as hustlers at all. Thus, of one hustler it was contemptuously remarked:

> He calls himself a hustler but he always dogs it for the cash. I guess his old lady supports him.

And of another:

> I've never seen him take down the cash. That movie turned him on to thinking he was a hustler, but he ain't. You could give him 12 on 30 [points in three-cushion billiards] and still have a lock. He should get a job.

At the top of the hierarchy are, of course, the players of outstanding skill. Although most hustlers can play any poolroom game well—and in addition many can, if need be, offer a sucker the handicap of shooting with the hand other than the one they normally use—they tend to specialize in one game or another. A hustler's standing among colleagues is based on this functional specialization, and he may be rated highly in one game but not in another (or not even thought of in connection with the other). Thus Wimpy, though he can play any pool game superbly, is known chiefly as the outstanding nine-ball hustler, Eddy Taylor (the Knoxville Bear) is rated best at bank pool, and so on. Some hustlers are noted for their ability to make a particularly difficult shot with great frequency and to win bets thereby; e.g., Don Willis is admired especially for making "wing shots" (in which you shoot at an object ball that is moving rapidly down the table away from you, and pocket it in a far corner).

There is by no means unanimity about who is the best in each specialty. Usually there are two or three candidates for that rating among the hustlers. For example, there is disagreement about who is the most adept specialist in the "I'll play you one-handed" routine; Lusitay has hustler partisans who claim he is best and so does Miami. And one can always get a good argument going among hustlers by asking who is the best one-pocket specialist, Ronnie Allen or Jersey Red or Marv Henderson.

Although hustlers specialize, most of them will, as noted above, play a game that's not their specialty if it is the only game the sucker will play. So if a hustler is a specialist in versatility, as it were, this also can confer status. It is in fact the basis of the extraordinary prestige that Boston Shorty enjoys among his colleagues. Hustlers do not rate him at the top in any specialty (except for a few who say he is probably the best at three-cushion billiards), but they are quick to point out that he is near the top in almost every specialty. By unanimous agreement, Boston Shorty is our country's best "all around" hustler.

It is assumed that every hustler knows how to "make a game," and this aspect of his work influences prestige rank among colleagues only if he is especially inept at it:

> X has got the heart and he's got the stroke. But he'll never be a good hustler, 'cause he's always giving away too many points. He's part sucker, that's what he is.

Another aspect of maladroitness in making a game was put down by Brooklyn Johnny, with whom I was watching a game in which hustler Y managed to eke out a win over a very tough non-hustler. I said something about hustler Y's great playing, and Johnny replied:

> But it's dumb. Look at the takedown [amount of cash] he got for it. It's dumb to make a game where you have to show the room your top speed for only $5.

Without exception, hustlers contend that "heart" (courage or toughness) is as essential to hustling as playing ability is. We saw earlier that they view it as basic to the job. The point here is that hustlers, in their preoccupation with it, often use judgments about "heart" to confer or withhold prestige. Some examples of such judgments that hustlers have made to me are these (each applies to a different hustler):

> You can't bet on A because you don't know how he's going to stand up for more than $20. No heart.

> Take B over there, thinks he's such a hotshot. But you'll never see him put up his own dough. He's got no heart, that's why. He's gotta have backing even when the game is a lock. B wouldn't play on his own dough unless the sucker had one foot in the grave, the other on a banana peel, and both arms in a cast.

> C don't have the heart for it. He only does okay when he gets out in front early.

> Weenie Beanie's got real heart. He's no locksman. A real strong gambler.

> I tell you one thing about Boston Shorty, the real great thing, is that the guy kisses icewater. He don't frighten out. One time I seen a game where somebody runs over 100 balls on him, and Shorty comes right back with 89 and out. It takes plenty heart to do that.

The *esprit de corps* of a colleague group, especially if it is a deviant group, tends to be strengthened by a well-developed hostility toward outsiders. But as we saw earlier, hustlers, for special reasons, do not have an elaborate ideology or strong feelings about this. They do, of course, sometimes speak contemptuously of outsiders; but in developing solidary feelings they rely much more on emphasizing the joys of hustling, talking of its virtues (such as autonomy and heart), rating each other, discussing its technology, telling tales of its heroes and villains, and so on. When a hustler says of hustling that "it beats working," his emphasis is not on putting down the workaday world; his primary meaning is, rather, a positive one—that hustling is infinitely more pleasurable than any other job he could find.

The fact that the hustler's work-place is to so great an extent also his leisure-place not only lessens his need for putting down the outside world, but at the same time increases those collegial interactions which foster *esprit de corps* by other means. One of those means, as should be obvious by now, is the use of an elaborate argot; I have placed my analysis of hustlers' argot in an appendix to this chapter, for reasons explained there.

Colleagueship involves an obligation to cooperate and rewards for doing so. Cooperation among hustlers takes several forms: (1) The main one, already discussed, is the cooperative swindle known as "dumping." (2) Often a hustler will tell a colleague about a fault he has noticed in the latter's game, although there appears to be no clearly defined collegial obligation to do this. (3) A clearly defined obligation, the strongest element in the hustlers' colleague code, has to do with regulating the competition for opponents: when a hustler has started to make a game (be it with a sucker or another hustler), any hustler who is a third party is not supposed to cut in with a better offer or otherwise queer the pitch; as previously noted, this sanction is observed not only by hustlers but by regular poolroom players generally. (4) When a hustler from out of town is cleaned out by some local hustler, the latter is obligated to give the former, on request, "get-out-of-town money." And whatever the winner's personal feelings about the loser, he doesn't fail to honor the request, so severe would be the castigation from his colleagues otherwise. (5) When a hustler is preparing for a road trip to towns he doesn't know, or hasn't visited in a long time, colleagues who have recently been to those places provide him with information on where the action is, who the best players are, what kind of cons they go for, and what their skill levels are. Conversely, when he returns from the road he fills in his colleagues with any new information he has gleaned on these matters.

More than a word needs to be said about the relationships between hustlers and professional players. The hustler and the professional have quite distinct occupational roles if we view them as ideal types, but empirically there is some overlap, especially today, and it leads to collegial relations between them that are extensive, complex, ambiguous and ambivalent.

The professional's income, years ago when professionalism paid well, derived mainly from tournament prizes, exhibition fees, endorsements of billiard products or representation of billiard supply firms, and teaching fees. Today, except for two or three top professionals, income from such sources is negligible. It is doubtful if even the current titleholder makes as much as $15,000 from them. (Compare this with Hoppe's 1925 estimate that the title was worth as much as $50,000 per year to whoever held it.) Professionals gain their income mostly from other occupations, especially managing a poolroom or owning a piece of one. One of these "other" occupations is hustling, and it appears that even in the earlier period many professionals also hustled on occasion. But it also appears that, except for a few professionals, they have done so infrequently. The great majority of professionals have often made big bets with opponents and spectators, but in situations where their skill levels were known to all concerned, i.e., not true hustling situations. In sum: many, possibly most, professionals have hustled—but seldom; and possibly a majority, certainly a large minority, of professionals either have never hustled at all or hustled only in early youth.

The very large majority of hustlers, on the other hand, have never tried to become professionals: They have stayed out of tournaments—in order, of course, to stay out of the limelight. At least, that's the reason most hustlers give. An additional reason, which they don't give, is that not many hustlers have been good enough to hold their own with the top professionals. However, if a hustler feels that his skill is already so well known that he has nothing much to lose by appearing in professional tournaments, and also feels that maybe he could win all the marbles, he will "go professional." And with the decline of potential income from hustling (see below), such feelings are becoming more common and the percentage of players in pro-

fessional tournaments who have long hustling backgrounds has
been going up.

Of course, if a hustler appears often in tournaments he
severely reduces his chances of true hustling. And should he
attain professional stardom, he effectively takes himself out
of hustling altogether, whether he wants to or not. For example,
as a result of his 1963 and later tournament victories, plus the
numerous paid public exhibitions he was able to give after
1963, Wimpy cannot really be a hustler any more—regardless
of what his current desire or self-conception may be. Today
there is scarcely a poolroom in America, and certainly none
with significant action, where he would not be recognized as
soon as he walked in the door. He can still play for big bets
(and does), but only with top players and, at that, by giving
them tremendous handicaps.

All of the above-mentioned blurring and criss-crossing of
occupational lines has led to some uneasy relations between
the professionals and the hustlers. (1) A good number of professionals who were never hustlers have been against hustlers
because the latter give the game a bad "image." There were
many such "respectable" professionals in the old days (Hoppe
is as good an example as any) and there are still some today
(e.g., Irving Crane). On the other hand, even these professionals
have a grudging respect for the skill of top hustlers and recognize that they are, after all, in the same sort of trade and have
the same love of the game. (2) Most of the professionals who
hustled a bit in their earliest days, or who have combined
professional play with occasional hustling for a significant part
of their careers, or who were basically hustlers before turning
professional, don't put down hustlers at all, hang around with
them, and in general find their company more congenial than
the company of "respectable" professionals. But at the same
time they are concerned to improve their chances of income
from professional play, and agree with the equipment manufacturers and poolroom owners that the best way of doing so
lies in improving the game's public "image"; as a result, they

will sometimes be publicly and calculatedly evasive about their hustling backgrounds. (3) A few (very few) players who formerly hustled not only have gone professional but, upon doing well at it, have gone respectable. As one would expect, they become more royalist than the king. For example, Willie Mosconi has been given to making contemptuous remarks in public about "hustlers" such as Wimpy—this despite the fact that Mosconi was himself quite a hustler in his youth. Needless to say, Mosconi's present contempt for hustlers is returned by them.

AN OCCUPATION IN DECLINE

Outsiders who saw *The Hustler* gathered that a good pool or billiard hustler can make big money or an excellent living by exercising his skills. In this matter as in some others, the movie falsified by offering past history as if it were the present. The days when the poolroom hustler could readily find non-hustlers willing to play for high stakes are long gone, and probably gone forever. Structural changes in American sporting life over the past thirty years have had disastrous consequences for the hustler (as for the professional player).

The major datum is, of course, the radical decline of American interest in pool or billiards. In the entire history of the United States, no other sport of nationwide appeal seems ever to have had such a proportionate drop in its popularity.[10] As we have seen in Chapter 1, the chief aspect of this decline is that today, even after the recent "revival," the number of American poolrooms is only about a fourth what it was in the

[10] Along with negative consequences for the hustler from decreased participation in pool or billiard playing, there has come disaster for the professional player in the form of decreased spectator interest. Today the final match of a professional tournament is lucky to draw 300–500 people, and the champion is lucky to draw 75 people to an exhibition. But it was not always thus. When Willie Hoppe played George Slosson for the championship in 1906, there were over 4,000 paying spectators (Cf. Hoppe, *Thirty Years of Billiards* [New York: Putnam, 1925], p. 103). And high spectator interest continued into the 1930's; see Mosconi's remark noted in Chapter 1, p. 30.

1920's. From talks with old-timers, I gather that the decline in action rooms has been proportionately even greater. For the hustler this means, among other things, that it is much harder to stay unknown. There are so few action rooms remaining that he cannot space his visits to them far enough apart to avoid damaging his reputation, i.e., to avoid getting too good a reputation. And, in addition, there are simply many less players and therefore many less bettors.

As if this were not enough, there has been a devastating shift (devastating for the hustler) in the ideology of the regular players who remain or enter the poolroom. They still adhere to the tradition that players should bet, but they bet far smaller amounts, absolutely as well as relatively, than they did thirty years ago. The decline of the game's hold on the American sporting imagination has meant that, even among the regular players, it is no longer considered the skill game on which to plunge. The big betting by non-hustlers on their playing skill has shifted to other sports. There are now many golf hustlers living high—several make upward of $25,000 a year—for they find plenty of cocky amateurs willing to stand heavy action. (Joe Louis is one such amateur. Part of the reason he went broke is that the golf hustlers took him so often.) And dozens of bowling hustlers do fairly well. But the pool or billiard hustler cannot make out. It is doubtful if today there are more than half a dozen poolroom hustlers who make even $7000 per year by their hustling.

Today, when the poolroom hustler plays a sucker, as often as not the action is "sociable," two or three dollars per game; the average (mean) action is perhaps $5. $10 or $15 is considered quite good action. $20 and up is uncommon, and games for as much as "half a yard" ($50) or more are downright rare. And, it must always be remembered, the hustler often has to go a good while between games that are true hustles for him. If he makes $90–$100 per week hustling, he's doing much better than average. True, almost any hustler will on the proper occasion tell of a big score he made off a sucker—say, $600 in one session. But if you pin him down as to how many times in the past few years he's made a score like that, it rarely turns out to be more than three or four times.

Games for $50 and more certainly do take place, on occasion, when hustlers play each other. (I have witnessed one series of games between two hustlers for $1,000 per game, and at least a dozen such series for $300–$800 per game.) But even here, really heavy action is uncommon; in hustler-vs.-hustler contests, the mean action is perhaps $15 or $20 per game. And in any case, though hustlers get a great kick out of the relatively big action when they play each other, they know that basically they are just taking in each other's washing.

There are certain peaks of these cannibalistic hustler-vs.-hustler contests: (a) Since 1961 there has been an annual tournament for hustlers in Johnston City, Illinois (pop. 3,900), with cash prizes but much more bet on the side between the players. It is sponsored by the Jansco brothers of that city, whose increased motel and bar business during the tournament makes up for the prize money they offer.[11] (b) When professional tournaments are held, hustlers from various cities come together as spectators and consequently adjourn to the local action room late at night for games with each other. (c) When word spreads that a poolroom has come up with a new local player willing to stand big action, hustlers flock to the room—and more often than not end up playing each other. For example, in 1962, New York City hustlers got the wire that a sucker in Lodi, New Jersey, would gamble heavily, and they began traveling across the river to seek him out; of a

[11] A good description of this scene is Tom Fox's "Hustler's Holiday in the Lion's Den," *Sports Illustrated,* Vol. 15 (December 4, 1961), pp. 53–56, 59–61; a grossly inadequate one is "Battle of the Hottest Sticks," *Sports Illustrated,* Vol. 18, No. 8 (February 25, 1963), pp. 32–37. Students of mass communications may be interested to know that in connection with the 1963 tournament a typical bit of TV fakery took place. Games between Luther Lassiter (Wimpy) and Eddy Taylor (The Knoxville Bear) were videotaped and later broadcast, on December 22, 1963, as a CBS *Sports Spectacular.* Although the tournament was for hustlers, CBS did everything possible to create the impression that it was not: the screen title was simply "World Pocket Billiard Championship," and the word "hustler" was never mentioned on the program.

weekend night there would often be eight or ten hustlers in Lodi, with only the one non-hustler willing to provide decent action, so naturally many hustler-vs.-hustler games developed to pass the time.

But neither the bigger action involved in hustler-vs.-hustler contests, nor their frequency, nor their great fascination, should lead us to blink the crucial fact that they constitute occupational cannibalism. No hustler seriously expects to make a living from playing other hustlers. He wants to find opponents whom he can truly hustle, and in this connection his never-ending problem is, Where's the big action?

A room where suckers play for decent money is so rare these days that when one does turn up, it is likely to be ruined through over-exploitation. An example: In 1962 a new poolroom opened in one of Cleveland's fancier suburbs, and the area's wealthy high school students began playing each other for sizeable stakes even though most of them scarcely knew how to hold a cue stick. Word got out and the hustlers descended—first the local hustlers from Cleveland's West 25th Street, and soon hustlers from all over the country. At its peak several hustlers were each pulling out as much as $400 per week from the room. But they tore it down; there were just too many hustlers taking too much money from too many kids, and mounting pressure from parents and police forced the room to close.

The professional three-cushion billiard player, Arthur Rubin, recently summed up the general situation as follows:

> In the old days when the hustler got too well known in his home town he just went on the road for a while. He did fine. Every town in America had its local champion willing to play for high stakes; and if the champion didn't have money himself, he always had plenty of backers willing to put it up. Today, the hustlers are more and more reduced to playing each other. And when that happens, that's not hustling—that's gambling.

The poolroom hustler, then, is a highly skilled man whose skills no longer find a lucrative outlet. His occupation, once quite rewarding financially, now can support very few people, and these barely. Why does the hustler hang on? How? What does he do if he can't? How did he come to be a hustler anyhow?

HANGING ON, CAREER CONTINGENCIES, AND RETIREMENT

The question, Why does the hustler hang on?, is somewhat misleading as applied to most hustlers. It implies that because hustling once was lucrative and now is not, today's hustler once had something valuable—a good living at his trade—that he now tries to "hang onto" after it has gone. But in my sample of *ca.* 59 hustlers (give or take a couple), 40 to 45 of them are under 50 years old and over half are under 40 years old. Now, if the good majority of hustlers are under 50, this means that they never had much to hang onto. The majority of today's hustlers entered hustling after its decline. The question to ask about them is, Why in the world did they become hustlers in the first place—and if they initially had false notions about its lucrativeness, why didn't they quit when they saw the reality (which indeed nearly all do see)? But let us look at the older group first.

The hustlers over 50 years old, who are truly "hanging on," are generally nostalgic, full of stories about famous matches and high stakes in the old days. It is only to be expected, I think, that a number of people who entered hustling when it was still big-time, or at least were in poolrooms when it was big-time, just won't give up hustling. What really needs explaining, it seems to me, is why so few such people are on today's hustling scene.

By all surmises, including their own, the active U.S. hustlers between 50 and 70 can comprise at the very most 5 per cent of living persons in this age group who once were hustlers. There must be hundreds of living ex-hustlers over 50 who loved the game, i.e., the whole lifestyle involved in the game, just as much as the old hustlers who haven't quit. If one can assume what strike me as two reasonable assumptions, that "love of the game" is no greater in the younger generation than in the older and that hustlers over 50 can draw sustenance from memories of the big-time that the young hustlers cannot, it remains to be explained why more old-timers are not still hustling.

The reader familiar with sports in general will know an obvious answer: if the good young hustler has trouble making ends meet, the old-timer's income from hustling must be worse yet—simply because, as we know from a variety of sports, one's skill level declines rapidly after reaching one's forties. But the obvious answer won't do. Pool and billiards are peculiar, nay unique, in that one can play at or very near one's top game well into old age—usually even to compensating fully for the hand tremors that often accompany old age. Of course, the older man doesn't have the stamina he once had, can't engage in all-night sessions very often. But otherwise, unless and until his sight becomes uncorrectable even with bifocals, he has no skill problem.

True, when the hustler's eyes no longer can be helped a great deal with glasses, he has had it. The ex-hustler Tugboat Whaley (so called because part of his con was pretending to be a tugboat captain) reports as follows:

> I'm 65. I haven't played for big stakes in 10 years. This game isn't like baseball—your legs don't give out, your eyes do. You don't lose your stroke. Your eyes go bad, you can't see the edge of the ball.[12]

However, it must be emphasized that the eyes of most hustlers are correctable or almost entirely correctable with glasses far into old age, and that consequently most hustlers can keep playing well.

An index of this peculiarity about the game is that the record time-span over which a player in any sport or game was still winning world championships is held by billiards: Willie Hoppe won his first world championship in 1906 and his last in 1952, forty-six years later (whereupon he retired, at the age of 65). It is true that Hoppe's skill level may have been

[12] Quoted from Tom Fox, *op. cit.,* p. 59.

unique.[13] But he was by no means unique in the number of years he was able to play his best. Nor can it be said that this is due to the particular varieties of the game that he played (balk-line and three-cushion billiards). For example, in the professional pocket billiard (pool) championship tournaments held between 1963 and 1965, there were four competitors over 55 years old out of a combined field of 23 different players in the three tournaments; i.e., four players over 55 were ranked among the best 23 players in the world—and one of these four was 69 years old. And I have played several opponents who, though not of championship calibre, were still superb players well past the age of 70.

Nor is there a decline in the old hustler's temperamental ability to feign less playing skill than he has, or in his ability to "make a game" or his other conning skills. Furthermore, his age does not make him suspect as someone whose accumulated knowledge and experience might prove too strong. On the contrary, the older hustler finds that once in a while his age, as such, helps him to hustle: sometimes an ignorant sucker will assume that a decrepit-looking old man couldn't possibly play a decent game any more, and finds out the hard way.

For some hustlers, as they get older, over-indulgence in alcohol becomes a severe problem. It has wrecked the careers both of hustlers and of professionals (e.g., to mention only the most famous among the dead, Ralph Greenleaf). However, alcoholism seems no more frequent among hustlers than in most other segments of our society.

Rather, the scarcity of old hustlers is explained by an aspect of the hustler's way of life today that is particularly hard to take in old age: today the periods in any hustler's career when he goes completely broke are more frequent and of longer duration. A young man may not be too shaken by the fact that once in a great while he can't even pay room rent in a fleabag hotel and has to grab his sleep in the poolroom for two or three days, or that he may get down to just one change

---

[13] And maybe not. Some old-timers claim that whenever Johnny Layton was even halfway sober (seldom), he beat Hoppe.

of clothes, for he knows that one decent hustle—bound to come along in a couple of days if he keeps sharp eyes out—will get him started again. But an older man finds himself looking for more security than that, finds himself less adaptable to the more frequent and more severe downturns that are a contingency of the hustling career today.

In addition, an indeterminate number of hustlers give up the poolroom life because they eventually get married and find, when they do, that this poses another great occupational problem. That is one reason why the great majority of career hustlers are career bachelors. Marriage is of course a contingency that can adversely affect careers in many occupations, as in, say, the case of the aspiring organization man whose spouse is not a proper organization wife; but in hustling, much more frequently and intensely than in most occupations, marriage precipitates a genuine career crisis.

Perhaps because bachelor ideology had so recently played a prominent part in his thinking, when the hustler does get married he is notably less successful than, say, a jazz musician, in finding a woman to put up with his irregular working hours. Whatever the cause may be, it appears that most women who marry hustlers can't or won't readily—or even unreadily—adjust to the erratic hours that hustling entails, or that are entailed when one wishes to watch or engage in games between hustlers (which, for reasons already indicated, take place mostly between the hours of 1:00 and 6:00 A.M.). Instances of such difficulties are frequently told in the hustling world, being cited most often, of course, by the bachelor majority as reason enough for their continued bachelorhood. Apart from erratic hours as such, the small and unpredictably fluctuating nature of the hustler's income poses an equally severe marriage-vs.-career problem, one that only a few hustlers have been able to ease by finding wives who will work steadily while they (the husbands) continue hustling.

Some hustlers solve this career crisis by eventually walking out on the wife; others solve it by eventually walking out on the poolroom. The latter solution appears to be more frequent, though how much more so I do not have enough data to say.

It is reasonable to speculate—though again I have no data —that some decades ago a hustler's marriage did not pose such a critical problem for him. In the old days hustlers had much more opportunity for good action with suckers in day-time and early evening hours (as opposed to today's frequently fruitless hunt during such hours), far lesser need to play each other, and consequently both greater choice of working hours and greater dependability of income.

The twin factors discussed above—crises posed by financial insecurity in old age and by marriage—strongly suggest that today's young hustlers, as they get older, will also show a very high dropout rate.

Hustlers who retire when young sometimes return to the poolroom for visits, to see friends or watch contests. But the older hustlers who drop out, and the young retired hustlers as they get older, tend to abandon the poolroom world entirely. Among the many old men who hang around or work in pool-rooms, there are few former hustlers.

Perhaps the best known of such former hustlers is Carl Zingale, now 70, whose monicker in the poolroom world is Cue Ball Kelly (an illustration, incidentally, that it is not always safe to infer someone's ethnic origin from his ethnic monicker). He was hustling by the age of 10:

> I was what you might call on the hustle. The dough wasn't too bad for a kid and I figured that I could make more money this way than I could in school. There were many days that I would win three or four games and come home with my pockets jingling. . . . After a few years I suddenly realized that I wasn't the greatest pool player around. So I decided to start picking up some money by refereeing and booking games [professional games]. I've refereed for every top player in the past 40 years and I've also handled bookings for them.

Although Kelly has made a fair living from professional tournaments by alternately refereeing and entertaining the audi-ence with trick shots, the business really isn't big enough to support more than one such person in this manner (and even

Kelly has had rough going at times). Retired hustlers who want to stay around the game have to take ordinary jobs in the poolroom. If they are lucky, they end up with ownership or part ownership of a poolroom, but rarely are they that lucky. For the most part they face only ill-paid and dead-end poolroom jobs (desk man, sweeper) and as a result tend to drift out of the poolroom to other jobs that, although also unskilled, pay a bit better.

RECRUITMENT AND INDUCTION

Hustlers arise in all regions of the country, and in small cities as well as big ones. (But the decline in action rooms forces the small-town hustlers to move to one or another of America's big cities, and also means that road trips to small towns are far rarer than they were thirty years ago.) The only significant factor common to their backgrounds appears to be that of social class.

At least four-fifths of the hustlers in my sample are of lower-class origin, and those who are not come, by anybody's definition, from the lower reaches of the middle class. One index: with a solitary exception, none of the hustlers attended college (not even those who could have done so on the GI Bill), and probably over half of them, certainly well over a third, did not finish high school. Hustlers' origins are also, by and large, in keeping with ethnic succession in the lower class.[14] For example, most of the Jewish hustlers are over 55; and Puerto Rican hustlers, virtually unknown until ten or fifteen years ago, now are much in evidence among the younger hustlers (one is often reputed to be the best one-handed player in the country).

Hustlers are social deviants, in the sense that they gamble

[14] This holds as well for the origins of professional players; see Chapter 1, note 40. See also Dudley Kavanagh's prideful observation in 1869: "Ireland, the mother of the majority of billiard professionals. . . ." (Kavanagh, *The Billiard World* [N. Y.: Kavanagh & Decker, 1869], p. 45).

for a living and, in the process, violate societal norms of "respectable" work and of fair dealing (and do worse things, as will emerge presently). However, psychopathology as such has nothing to do with either the origin or maintenance of their hustling. Many a psychiatrically oriented observer might indeed find that hustlers as a group seem to show more mental disorder than people he knows in general, but this would be merely to say that his "in general" includes little acquaintance with the lower class, where, as several researchers have amply demonstrated, the burden of mental illness in our society mainly falls. As a matter of fact, hustlers as a group may well be psychologically healthier than those members of the lower class whose teens were spent in more respectable places than poolrooms; this would not be out of keeping with the data, reported by the Gluecks and others, which indicate that in lower-class neighborhoods of high delinquency the non-delinquents have higher neuroticism rates than the delinquents.

The causes relevant to hustling are not psychopathological but subcultural. In the context of American lower-class subcultures, hustlers are not nearly so "deviant" as they appear to the middle- or upper-class outsider. For one thing, in lower-class areas pool playing is a much commoner pastime and the poolroom is more frequently a neighborhood institution.

Secondly, the "social norms" that the hustler transgresses carry less weight in the lower class than elsewhere, and correspondingly the hustler is stigmatized less. After all, in lower-class subcultures the successful neighborhood racketeer or political thief is frequently admired, and hustlers *qua* hustlers are less violative of basic social norms than such people. Nor does the fact that hustling isn't a "steady job" carry in the lower class the stigma that it does elsewhere.

Thirdly, and crucially: hustling, notably unlike most American occupations, represents a career line that is almost completely open to members of the lower class, an occupation where social origin bars one neither from entry nor advancement.

I say "almost" completely open because there is some discrimination against Negroes—not, however, by white hustlers, but by white poolroom owners. Even so, racial integration in the poolroom has been significantly in advance of that in the world outside it. Two examples: (a) Negroes were an accepted part of the Times Square poolroom scene by the early 1940's, in the days when their patronage of Times Square movies was discouraged and they simply couldn't get served by most restaurants in the area. (b) When I visited Cleveland in 1963, its public places were still so segregated that even in the action poolrooms on West 25th Street, the owners would pull the "club members only" routine to keep Negroes out. But the white hustlers objected strongly to this practice, and, moreover, would frequently travel to the Negro section for matches with the better Negro players (hustlers or otherwise). At the main Negro action room, on 105th and Massey, it was expected that white players would drop in, and quite okay for them to do so.[15] This relative lack of anti-Negro discrimination by white hustlers is part of a larger phenomenon: the social bonds uniting members of any deviant subculture tend to override race prejudice in large degree, and thus nearly every such subculture is more racially integrated than is "respectable" society.[16]

Hustling, then, is fully open to lower-class whites, and more open to lower-class Negroes than are most jobs. Except

[15] During the course of this study Howard Becker interviewed for me a San Francisco hustler, Harry the Russian, who indicated that in recent years the decline of pool hustling has made it more difficult for a white hustler to move in Negro neighborhoods without being rousted by police. Harry the Russian says that when he went into the Fillmore (the Negro section of San Francisco) in the old days, the police knew he was there to hustle pool and let him alone, but now they assume he is there to score for drugs or girls, stop him, and make him explain his presence.

[16] America's most racially integrated deviant subculture is probably the homosexual. For example, the homosexuals' annual "drag ball," held on Halloween in several cities, is one of our country's chief interracial events. And the Negro community knows it; e.g., at the Chicago drag ball I attended in 1955, the guest of honor was America's second most powerful Negro political leader, U.S. Congressman William Dawson. (It perhaps needs explaining that Halloween has a latent function as a sort of homosexual national holiday because at that time transvestites can go forth in women's clothing ["drag"] without fear of arrest. Mardi Gras has a similar function for homosexuals.)

for the discrimination faced by Negroes, success depends strictly on individual skills. And, still more importantly, it depends on the kind of skills that a lower-class youth has a good chance to acquire—unlike, say, the skills whose acquisition depends on parental encouragement of reading.

In hustling, nepotism or knowing people who are "well connected" counts for naught; the manly virtue of self-reliance counts for plenty. Hustling distributes its rewards strictly on the basis of individual talent and hard work, thus fulfilling two cardinal tenets of the Horatio Alger "myth" (as distinguished from the reality of the Alger novels themselves, where, as the late Richard Wohl noted, fortuitous events play a key role in success).

All in all, for a number of lower-class youths, hustling as a possible ladder of social ascent seems very real. As Boston Shorty put it to me: "If I hadn't got interested in pool when I was a kid, I might have ended up a bum or in jail."

The induction process in hustling has remained unchanged over the decades; it is the same for today's newcomer as it was for the old-timer. The difference is only that far fewer youths enter the career these days because of the decreased chances to earn good money from it. But some continue to enter; in our larger cities, each year the hustling scene reveals a few new young faces.

In general the process goes like this: Hustlers, even those who finished high school, played truant from school often, and in so doing found themselves in poolrooms much more frequently than either their classmates or their fellow-truants. Since the development of pool or billiard skill is, at least in the first several years of play, largely a matter of the number of hours one practices, they quickly developed superiority over their age-mates and were able to earn some fair change thereby. Naturally they wanted to keep a good thing going, and in the process many dropped out of school entirely, while nearly all passed up job experience and training; almost without thinking about it they became hustlers, as much by drift as by decision. The only significant exception to this general line of development is that some hustlers, now in their forties, had an extra reason for spending much of their youth in poolrooms, namely, their teens were depression years when there were no jobs around.

Because in hustling there is neither a formal entrance requirement nor formal recognition of entry (no examination, license, *rite de passage,* union membership, etc.) and, especially, because the poolroom tradition that all players should bet makes it nearly impossible to recall (or even to distinguish at the time) any hustling analogue of one's "first real job," the transition from non-hustler to hustler status is smooth and almost imperceptible to the person involved. The transition never seems to involve a conscious decision to *become* a hustler, but rather a recognition that one already *is* a hustler, and is good at it. Here is a typical response to my queries about entry:

> How I got to be a hustler? Well it wasn't any special deal, you know. When I was a kid around 14 I was shootin' pool for money like the other kids, only I got to be the best, and after a while you can't get a game if you let on how good you are. And pretty soon I was beating lots older guys, 'cause right away I come up with a real good stroke, you know. And me with my baby face, they didn't know what was happenin' until I took down the cash. I was better at hustlin' pool than anything else, so I figured I would keep on doin' it.

And here is an account by the man sometimes regarded as America's best one-pocket hustler, Jersey Red:

> I thank them, every one of them down there in the New YMCA. That's where I got my start. I hustled for Cokes and change, and if they had some that folded and some nerve, I would unfold it for them. I started in there when I was 13 and when I was 14 I got my stroke. I got my stroke and learned to count [pocket the balls]. I beat every kid in the Y and then I started lookin' around. I just kept looking.[17]

Although the hustler's career decision—if one can call it that—may come late, acquisition of the playing skills requisite

[17] Quoted from Dale Shaw, *op. cit.,* p. 91.

to hustling must start early. Every first-rate pool or billiard
player, hustler or not, began playing regularly no later than
his early teens.[18]

Once embarked in the hustling life, hustlers prefer to stay
in it: it's exciting, it has a tradition and ideology that can
make them feel heroic, it's fun (the game is enjoyable as such),
it's not routine, and so on. The point is that these characteristics of the occupation, appealing as they might be to, say,
the readers of this book, are still more appealing to lower-
class youths. The hustling career partakes deeply, often passionately, of every one of the orientations that Walter Miller
finds to be distinctive "focal concerns" of American lower-class
subcultures: trouble (with the law), smartness (in the sense of
being able to con and of being no one's dupe), excitement,
fate, toughness ("heart"), and autonomy.[19]

The existence of such orientations in hustling has tremendous positive consequences both for the entry of lower-class
youths and for their continuing with the career in the face of
frequent financial adversity. And on top of all that, "love of
the game" is an important element in the makeup of most
hustlers—the same kind of "hangup" on a game, as such,
that one finds in chess bums, tennis bums, *et al.* (and that is
the main basis of my relationship with hustlers). Thus, although
numerous problems confront the hustler, "alienation" from his
work is emphatically not one of them. It is small wonder that
when asked why he stays in the occupation, many a hustler
replies: "It beats working."

However, despite the fact that the typical hustler supports
only himself and pays no income tax, it is frequently hard
to make ends meet, and sometimes impossible. The rate of
failure is high, and the hustler knows it. For example, when a
hustler *un*intentionally misses a shot, sometimes he will curse
himself with the exclamation "Get a job!," whereby he recog-

[18] See Chapter 1.
[19] Cf. Walter Miller, "Lower Class Culture as a Generating Milieu
of Gang Delinquency," *Journal of Social Issues,* Vol. XIV (1958), pp.
5–19.

nizes, albeit ironically, that he is in a very tough racket where only the best survive and he may not make it.

Some hustlers do indeed give up when still young. It is not uncommon for a young hustler who hasn't been in the poolroom for a while to say, when he finally does show up to see his friends and is queried about his absence, "I'm retired." But most hustlers, once they have entered the career, stick it out tenaciously for a number of years. The action (in all senses) provides too many pleasures for them to worry that much about being broke.

But sooner or later even the best and most determined hustler finds that if he is to keep hustling he must, at least on occasion, obtain other sources of income. That is, he finds that if he is not to retire, he must moonlight. In many cases, when hustlers are moonlighting, the major share of their income derives from the latter source. Sometimes the hustler gets to depend on, or actually to like, his moonlighting job, and moonlights permanently to all intents and purposes.

MOONLIGHTING

The purpose of moonlighting is not merely to provide more income but to provide it in a way that allows you to keep your primary job, the one you prefer. The job the hustler takes, therefore, is one that allows him to hustle. Such jobs fall into two types:

(1) Poolroom-based. The hustler may take a job as a desk clerk, general handyman, lunch-counter man, etc., in the poolroom. More often, he will engage in some illegal activity that either can be headquartered in the poolroom or, because its "working hours" are short and sporadic, permits him to hang around the poolroom most of the time. His lower-class origin, his lack of legitimate job training, the availability of contacts in the poolroom for criminal jobs, the ethic of hustling life— all these facilitate taking criminal jobs when moonlighting.

He may moonlight at being a booster, or fence, or drug

pusher, or loan shark, or numbers runner, or forger, or burglar, or bookie, etc. Several hustlers in my sample are also
skilled card cheats ("mechanics," in the argot). Three hustlers
are also pimps, have women who "hustle" in the usual sense.
(One has rather high poolroom status because his girl always
gets at least $50 per trick.) At least three members of the
sample, perhaps more, are "heavy men" in their moonlighting
roles, i.e., their moonlighting involves the use or potential use
of armed violence.

Among hustlers who have moonlighted at crimes which
society defines as more serious than hustling itself, the frequency of participation varies all the way from the hustler
who has undertaken such activity only once or twice to the
hustler who undertakes it more or less continuously. My point
is that over half the hustlers have, apparently, undertaken
such moonlighting at least once.

But the point as far as the hustler is concerned is that such
a job allows him to hustle. In either kind of poolroom-based
job, legal or illegal, the hustler is on hand to grab whatever
action might present itself.

(2) Not poolroom-based. A job based in the poolroom is of
course preferable to any other kind of moonlighting; it allows
the hustler to stay in the poolroom all or nearly all the time.
But if the hustler wanting to moonlight can't get such a job, he
tries to make sure that the job he takes at least permits him to
drop into the poolroom often. It can't be an office or factory or
retailing job, for these would tie him down to another location.
It has to let him move around the city, and have somewhat
flexible hours if possible, so that he can spend at least some
time checking on the action in poolrooms. Among such jobs:
window washer, outside salesman, cab driver.

A few (very few) hustlers have become wealthy from outside activities. One made oil investments that paid off; another
is associated with racketeers in a lucrative vending machine
business; another is a major bookmaker; another owns restaurants; another has made a fortune cheating at cards; and
another has, at this writing, six prostitutes working for him.

POOL HUSTLER:

ALIASES: John Bemis, Henry Milton Bradley, Patrick Bradley, John Frank Fitzpatrick, Charles C. Garrett, Melvin C. Horton, William L. Johnson, Lee Frank Rae, W. L. Wells and others

BACKGROUND AND METHOD OF OPERATION

Bradley allegedly has passed worthless checks at retail stores, gas stations, hotels and motels throughout the United States. Bradley frequently used the name John F. Fitzpatrick and traveled mainly by automobile. He is known in pool halls as a "pool hustler." He has been convicted of interstate transportation of stolen property, forgery and attempting to commit a felony. BRADLEY REPORTEDLY CARRIES A .38 CALIBER REVOLVER IN WAISTBAND OF HIS TROUSERS. CONSIDER ARMED AND DANGEROUS.

DESCRIPTION

Age: 50, born June 16, 1915, Washington, D.C.

Height: 6' to 6'1"

Weight: 305 to 320 pounds

Build: Large

Hair: Brown, graying

Eyes: Blue

Complexion: Ruddy

Race: White

Nationality: American

FBI No.: 4,111,234

F.P.C.: 19 L 13 R 101 15 M 1 R 100

Occupations: Billiard parlor employee, guard, laborer, insurance agent, private investigator, salesman

Scars and Marks: Scar over left eye, scar left knee

Federal warrants were issued March 4, 1965, and May 28, 1965, at Roanoke, Virginia, and Greensboro, North Carolina, respectively, charging Bradley with causing fraudulent checks to be transported in interstate commerce (Title 18, U. S. Code, Section 2314).

PLEASE FURNISH ANY INFORMATION WHICH MAY ASSIST IN LOCATING THIS INDIVIDUAL TO THE NEAREST DIVISION OF THE FBI AS LISTED ON THE BACK OF THIS NOTICE.

But poolroom hustling remains their true love. For example, the hustler grown rich from vending machines spends two days a week looking after his business and five days a week in poolrooms. It is entirely possible that a few hustlers who somehow struck it rich from moonlighting may have thereupon retired from hustling, but I have never heard of such. There are, of course, a number of people who retired from hustling and then did well in the other occupations they entered, e.g., the baseball pitcher Bo Belinsky.[20]

THE OCCASIONAL HUSTLER

So far, except for noting that professional players have hustled, I have considered only the hustling done by hustlers, i.e., persons whose primary occupational identification is with pool or billiard hustling and who engage in it as a full-time career whenever they are not forced to moonlight. There are, however, a number of casual laborers in the field.

Over 99 per cent of the more-or-less regular adult poolroom players are not hustlers. Only a small minority of them are even good enough to hustle. But a minority of this minority, such as myself, do hustle on occasion, e.g., "stall" and "lemon" so as to keep opponents playing and betting. However, their primary occupational identification lies elsewhere. I am rather untypical of such persons not only because of my middle-class background, but because most of them have jobs which allow them much more time in the poolroom—are traveling salesmen, professional criminals, holders of political sinecures, etc. The late jazz pianist Jelly Roll Morton was an occasional hustler of this kind.[21]

[20] On Belinsky's hustling background see, for example, Walter Lee Jackson, "Bo Belinsky: Baseball's 'Beau'," *Modern Man,* Vol. 12, No. 11 (May, 1963), pp. 36–38, 51.
[21] In his talking and singing autobiography, recorded at the Library of Congress in 1938, Morton has left some fascinating recollections of his pool hustling in the years 1900–1908. Listen to the Jelly Roll Morton Library of Congress recordings, as follows: volume 5, *Georgia Skin Game,* Riverside RLP 9005 (side 1, "Aaron Harris" bands 1 and 2); volume 9, *Jack the Bear,* Riverside RLP 9009 (side 1, "Jack the Bear" bands 1, 2, and 3; side 2, "Alabama Bound" bands 3 and 4).

However, virtually none of these persons is as skilled as the typical hustler. They hustle very little, not merely because they wish to do so less often than the hustler but because they must be more cautious than he in picking opponents. They account for only a tiny fraction of all hustled games, perhaps 1 per cent.

Secondly, of the many players who are high school students not yet entered into society's occupational structure, some hustle. A few of the best will eventually become hustlers by trade, though most will not. They hustle their age-mates primarily, as few are skilled enough to beat the more experienced players. They account, I would guess, for perhaps 2 or 3 per cent of all hustled games.

A third group, however, accounts for quite a significant percentage of hustled games, at a guess about 15 per cent.[22] This group consists of people who are no longer students but who have no occupational identity whatever. When indicating how he makes his living, such a person may say that he "scuffles," or that he "gets by" by doing "a little of this and a little of that." His varied activities are more often than not illegal. Sometimes he may say that he "hustles," but he means this in the generalized slang sense that he undertakes any short-term activity for a fast buck.[23] Pool-playing skill is merely one element of his armamentarium. He may be hustling at pool one night, in a crooked dice game the next, hustling his own ass in a gay bar the next, and so on. It is my impression—though the sample is too small to permit sure generalization—that this group shows a greater incidence of mental disorder than other poolroom groups and also that Negroes are significantly over-represented in it.

[22] N.B. that all the remarks above about "percentages" of hustled games are strictly guesses, though informed guesses.

[23] A valuable autobiography of one such "hustler" or "scuffler," transcribed from tape-recorded interviews, is Henry Williamson's *Hustler* (New York: Doubleday, 1965). Its accounts of pool hustling are at pp. 73, 93 ff., and 156 ff. Williamson's vocational drifting (or versatility) is entirely criminal and concentrates on felonies, chiefly armed robbery. Pool hustling, as it merely breaks misdemeanor laws against gambling, constitutes his nearest approach to a legitimate occupation. For the life history of another such "hustler," see Edwin Lemert, *Social Pathology* (New York: McGraw-Hill, 1951), pp. 332–37.

THE HUSTLER IN HISTORY

Although the techniques of deception that can be used in a gambling game are modified by the game's social context, these techniques flow fundamentally, as we noted at the beginning, from the inner structure of the game itself. Thus we might reasonably suspect analogues of the modern hustler's techniques to have been used in the earliest forms of billiard games.

But it doesn't help much to state, as a *terminus a quo* for hustling, the date when something like billiards first was played, because nobody has demonstrated what that date might be. Billiard historians have indeed proposed several dates and places for the origin of the game; however, as indicated in Chapter 1, such historians are hopelessly incompetent. (Many of them, for example, state that billiards was known in ancient Egypt, the "evidence" being that Shakespeare has Cleopatra say "Let us to billiards.") Until research on the subject that I have under way is completed—if my hunch is right, it will demonstrate that billiards began in fifteenth-century France—we had best skip this matter and turn from the origin of billiards to the question of what the historical record might have to say, if anything, about billiard players' conscious use of hustling techniques as such. And it does say something.

The earliest evidence of hustling I have found so far (let me reiterate that my research is not completed) reveals that not only hustling techniques, but the poolroom hustler as a distinct occupational type, had arisen in Europe by the time of the Industrial Revolution. The basic strategies and tactics of present-day hustling were adumbrated by the workers of *ancien regime* France.

To be sure, there were differences because the structure of billiard games and the superstructure of betting relationships differed somewhat from today's practice. But by the 1770's, in the poolrooms of Paris, there had developed clear-cut equivalents of today's stalling, lemoning, and dumping. There had also emerged the professional gambler who lived off his bets on hustlers, the prototype of today's backer, and indeed his was more often a full-time occupational role than that of the hustler.

In addition, the subtle art of "making a game" was highly developed, the principal difference being that in pre-revolutionary Paris, non-playing bettors participated fully in arranging the handicap terms of a match. And the eighteenth-century hustler had a remarkably modern bag of ancillary short-con routines, e.g., he too would pretend to be upset by an unlucky break and to be badly thrown off his game thereby.[24]

A number of modern hustlers, like some other regular players, have so great a love of the game that for all their lack of formal education they show much genuine interest in and knowledge of billiard history. Not only are they more historically minded than other deviant groups, not only has much material written by billiard historians—true and untrue—filtered down to them, but they have preserved a good bit of billiard history and playing technique by means of a long oral tradition. For example, it was from a hustler that I first learned exactly how the structure of the game played by Phelan and Seereiter in 1859 differed from today's game.[25] Or, to give an example from playing technique, many refinements and extensions of the mathematical systems for calculating three-cushion billiard shots have never been published, but have been simply passed on orally from one generation of players—including hustlers—to the next.[26] So it did not seem to me fantastic on the face of it to wonder if modern American hustlers knew anything of their European predecessors. I found that a few hustlers and also

[24] I take all this material on Parisian hustling in the 1770's from the eyewitness account of Restif de la Bretonne; see his *Les Nuits de Paris* (Paris: Hachette, 1960), as follows: "Les Billards: Acteurs," pp. 116–19; "Suite du Billard: Le Prête-Nom," pp. 119–22; "Suite du Billard: La Revanche," pp. 124–26; "Suite: Le Coup de Grace," pp. 127–30.

[25] On the significance of this game, see Chapter 1.

[26] The fullest published information on mathematical systems for three-cushion billiards can be found in Willie Hoppe, *Billiards as It Should be Played* (Chicago: Reilly and Lee, 1941) pp. 64 ff. But full as it may be, it is only a small part of what the best older students of the subject know, use in their playing, and pass on orally to younger players.

some non-hustlers did indeed have knowledge, or folklore, about hustlers who were active before they were born, but that this material extended neither beyond the 1890's nor beyond America.

That the oral tradition, strong though it is, knows nothing of American hustlers earlier than the 1890's doesn't rule out the possibility that there were such hustlers. But it led me to think that in comparing modern American hustling with early European predecessors, I was probably seeing "history" where none existed, that what really was involved was not cultural diffusion but independent invention. Such facts as I have been able to gather support this latter interpretation.

Before one can talk of cultural diffusion one must demonstrate cultural contact. For example, it would be absurd to suggest that the syncopation in Negro jazz derives from syncopation's prior appearance in Beethoven's Ninth Symphony (absurd because the slaves didn't go to Beethoven concerts), but sensible to suggest that it derives from the syncopation in West African music (sensible because the slaves did come from West Africa). Now, billiards did not come to America from the sort of poolrooms and persons described by Restif de la Bretonne, nor from similar milieux in England. All the evidence we have indicates that it diffused from the British tradition of upper-class private playing (see Chapter 1). Public tables made their appearance in America very soon afterward, but that was a native development rather than an importation, i.e., private playing by the American upper class quickly "trickled down" to become public playing by the middle and lower classes, at first on tables in taverns and inns, later in poolrooms as such.

Moreover, if we consider Michael Phelan's 1850 comment about the number of public tables in earlier days (p. 35), it is obvious that there wouldn't have been much point for American hustlers to have existed before, say, 1825, because there wouldn't have been anything like the "opportunity structure" that existed in the Paris of Restif. And the *New York Times* correspondent in Detroit in 1859, reporting on preparations for the Phelan-Seereiter match, wrote that in addition to the good players who had come from all over the country to see the contest, there were also in town "a great many black-legs, sharpers, and the like, and probably some pickpockets," but significantly didn't mention hustlers (neither "black-leg" nor "sharper" had that meaning in America).[27]

The lack of hustlers in 1859 wasn't due to any lack of poolrooms or players; there were plenty of both by then. But one key element of the opportunity structure was still missing: heavy action. The poolroom tradition that all players should bet on themselves—not merely on those battling it out for a championship—was just getting started. In 1850, Michael Phelan correctly noted that billiards was

> sometimes desecrated to purposes of gambling . . . . yet, as a general thing, playing for money is prohibited in the Billiard Rooms and Saloons of this country; in truth, it is a very unusual circumstance to hear, that money is wagered on Billiards at present.[28]

And in 1869 Dudley Kavanagh could still write, with absolute honesty and only slightly less accuracy, that

> Betting on billiards is not common in this country between the players engaged. In England a game is scarcely thought to be worth playing unless for a stake, however small. This is also the custom in Continental Europe. The very little betting which is done here (besides large bets on professional matches) is for the expense of the game and the accompanying refreshments.[29]

But note that Kavanagh says there were "large bets on professional matches." Since that would mark the true beginning in America of the requisite opportunity structure, it is where one would expect to find the first recorded instance of American hustling—and where one does find it: the early professionals Carme and Rudolphe, in a match played on November 18, 1868, acted in collusion to dump the bettors.[30] American hustling was started by the professional players themselves.

As more and more of the ordinary players began betting on their own matches in addition to the professionals' matches,

---

[27] *New York Times,* April 14, 1859, *Supplement,* [p. 2], col. 3.
[28] Michael Phelan, *Billiards Without a Master* (New York: D. D. Winant, 1850), p. 7.
[29] Dudley Kavanagh, *op. cit.,* p. 67.
[30] *Ibid.,* p. 32.

hustling arose as an occupation distinct from professional play. For example, one player's recollection (published in 1914) of billiards in South Michigan during the period 1860 to 1890, describes the emergence of hustlers "along near the end of this period," and tells how rumors of a fine young player in Plainville, Michigan, "attracted the attention of what today would be called the 'sharks' in Chicago, Detroit, and other cities." [31] It would seem that the earliest date for American hustlers preserved in today's oral tradition is not far off the mark after all.

By about 1890, then, through an independent line of development, American poolrooms had become what their French and English predecessors had long been: full-fledged action rooms, with suckers ready to plunge on their own skill and hustlers ready to take them. The words of wisdom for players in E. White's British billiard book of 1807 (which, as I indicated, is probably swiped from a French book), by the 1890's applied to America too:

> No billiard room of any notoriety is free from men who are gamesters by profession, and who are constantly in waiting to catch the ignorant and unsuspecting, who occasionally drop in, from motives either of curiosity or amusement; and by constant practice they acquire a degree of dexterity, that enables them to obtain an easy advantage over the generality of their opponents. Their grand object is to conceal their skill from their adversary, and to accommodate their play to his, in such a manner, as to appear to obtain the conquest more in consequence of good fortune than good play. In order to effect this, they . . . chiefly depend upon those strokes, the intent of which are apparent only to those who are intimately acquainted with the minutiae of the game. They generally suffer their adversary to gain some few games . . . but in the end, it is well for him indeed, if he escape being fleeced of all the ready money he may happen to have about him.[32]

That's what the hustler did, and does.

[31] George Hersch, "Billiards in South Michigan from 1860 to 1890 (Second Installment)," *Billiards Magazine,* Vol. 1, No. 11 (February, 1914), pp. 17–19.

[32] E. White, *A Practical Treatise on the Game of Billiards* (London: W. Miller, 1807), p. 2.

CONCLUSIONS

Throughout this study I have used a special orientation toward the material, an orientation not generally found in other studies of people who make their living from illegal work.[33] If, nevertheless, I have managed to make sociological sense out of the data, then it follows that the special orientation provides the most significant lesson of this study for the future of criminological research. The lesson is this: criminologists stand to lose little and gain much in the way of sociological understanding if, when studying people dedicated to an illegal occupation, they will overcome their fascination with the "illegal" part long enough to focus on the "occupation" part. After all, any theory of illegal occupations can be but a special case, albeit an important one, of general occupational theory.

Criminologists, following the lead of the late Edwin Sutherland, recognize that one hallmark of the career criminal—be he engaged in major crime or, like the hustler most of the time, in violating generally unenforced criminal law—is that the illegal activity in question constitutes his regular job.[34] Yet their researches seem thoroughly untenanted by what occupational sociologists have learned about how to look at someone's regular job. An example: one of the best recent criminological studies of a specific type of career criminal is Roebuck and Cadwalleder's research on Negro armed robbers.[35] But for all its useful findings—and there are plenty—the study is also a

[33] I know of only one other study of an illegal occupation that has an orientation similar to mine: James Bryan's "Apprenticeships in Prostitution," *Social Problems,* Vol. 12, No. 3 (Winter, 1965), pp. 287–97. Howard Becker's *Outsiders* (New York: Free Press of Glencoe, 1963), although it does not deal with illegal work, is the pioneering application of this framework to the sociology of deviance; Becker employs it to analyze avocational lawbreakers (marihuana users) and people whose work is legal but who are nevertheless stigmatized (jazz musicians).

[34] See, for example, Marshall Clinard, *Sociology of Deviant Behavior,* rev. ed. (New York: Holt, Rinehart & Winston, 1963), pp. 210–11.

[35] Cf. Julian Roebuck and Mervyn Cadwalleder, "The Negro Armed Robber as a Criminal Type," *Pacific Sociological Review,* Vol. 4 (Spring, 1961), pp. 21–26.

story of missed research opportunities because it proceeds with blissful inattention to what sociology has had mainly to say about one's "career" and its relation to other matters.

What is especially surprising about criminology's neglect of these occupational aspects as such, is that people dedicated to an illegal occupation actually *tell* the criminologist these aspects are central in their thinking and, moreover, under the right conditions can be observed to behave in accord with their statements on the matter. Thus one would think that the criminologist, even if he had read little or no occupational theory, would become inescapably aware of its possible relevance just as soon as he began seriously to study a career-oriented deviant. (This is in fact how I first became aware of its possible relevance—although not, as it happened, out of acquaintance with hustlers but out of acquaintance with a burglar.)

But the criminologist doesn't reach such awareness because he doesn't appreciate the career deviant's statements indicating the centrality of occupational concerns. (For example, when a professional criminal describes himself as being "like a businessman" or "just in a different line of business," the criminologist takes this to be merely a rationalization. It is a rationalization all right, but it is by no means merely that, and often it is not even primarily that.) The reason the criminologist doesn't appreciate such statements is that he doesn't confirm them from his own observation. And the reason he doesn't confirm them from his own observation is that he doesn't study the deviant under proper conditions. As for what the proper conditions are and why the criminologist doesn't avail himself of them, that is the subject of the next chapter.

As to the possible gain for criminology in the orientation I suggest, consider, for example, one theoretical implication of what the hustler often does when he needs additional sources of income. It suggests the possibility that many of the data criminologists refer to by rubrics such as "the occasional criminal" or "occasional crime" would be more sharply conceptualized and better understood under the heading "crime as moonlighting." This is for two reasons. First, as soon as we think of crime in this way, it becomes clearer that much serious crime (e.g., bank robbery) is undertaken by people who are neither "mentally ill" nor "white-collar criminals" nor oriented to serious crime as a career nor even oriented to milder crime as a career (unlike the hustler), but who are employed in and identify with perfectly legitimate lower-class jobs, get way behind in their bills, and see temporary or "one shot" criminal activity as a way to get solvent without giving up their regular jobs. It would also become clearer that the same often holds true for milder crimes, e.g., non-victim crimes such as prostitution, which is frequently undertaken in a moonlighting way by typists, salesgirls, and the like. (Moonlighters in prostitution are so frequent that the professionals have even developed argot terms for them; they are called "weekenders" by the professional prostitutes in Las Vegas and "party girls" by the professionals in New York.)

Second, a major precondition of moonlighting, according to Wilensky, is the existence of "occupations and industries on flexible work schedules which provide opportunity for part-time help," [36] and more recent analysis by labor economists confirms the point: "The industries in which 'moonlighters' found their second jobs were typically those providing opportunities for part-time work." [37] Most crime fits these descriptions perfectly. Indeed, one of the most genuinely appealing things about crime to career criminals and part-timers alike— though one would hardly gather this from the criminology texts —is that for most crimes the working hours are both short and flexible.

Criminological research informed by the orientation I suggest would also, of course, turn up material both new and germane to the sociological study of work as such. In the present study, I have noted some such findings in the section on col-

[36] Cf. Harold Wilensky, "The Moonlighter: A Product of Relative Deprivation," *Industrial Relations,* Vol. 3, No. 1 (October, 1963), pp. 106 ff.

[37] Forrest Bogan and Harvey Hamel, "Multiple Jobholders in May 1963," *Monthly Labor Review* (U.S. Dept. of Labor), Vol. 87, No. 3 (March, 1964), p. 249.

leagueship. Here I would like to point out certain other findings that seem to have no analogue in the literature of occupational sociology.

(1) The work situation. We saw that the hustler must be not
only a skilled player, but that he must be skilled at pretending
not to have great playing skill. The latter requirement is one
thing that distinguishes him from the usual con man (who often,
on the contrary, feigns more expertise that he has). And it also
distinguishes him from the usual professional gambler. The latter indeed sometimes pretends to be other than he is and dis-
claims real skill ("I guess I'm just lucky tonight"), but he relies
basically on playing skill alone, or else on a combination of
playing with cheating skill—being able to switch dice in and
out of a game, or to deal seconds or thirds or bottom cards,
etc. Pretending to lack of skill is not a basic requirement of
the gambler's job, as it is for the hustler. As far as I know,
this hustling reliance on competence at feigning incompetence
is unique, and nowhere treated in the occupational literature.

(2) Careers. Certain occupational roles require youthfulness
by definition (e.g., acting juvenile parts), and thus enforce unusually early retirement.[38] In certain other occupations (airline
pilots, for example) age-related career contingencies also force
early retirement. It is common to cite competitive sports or
games requiring high physical skills as examples of this type—
but pool or billiard playing doesn't fit the pattern. And because
such faulty generalizing about sports occurs not only among

[38] The earliest documented retirement of this kind I have run
across is the following: "Chattanooga, Jan. 7 (UPI)—Chris Haley retired from county government service yesterday at the age of 9. Chris
had been drawing names for Hamilton County grand jurors since 1959.
The law requires such tasks to be performed by children under 10. The
boy will be 10 in March." From the New York *Daily News,* January 8,
1964, p. 42.

occupational sociologists but among the populace at large, sometimes old age actually helps the hustler in his con.

In textbooks and treatises on the sociology of work, the attention paid to the moonlighter is notable for its scantiness. To the extent that occupational sociologists have studied the subject, they agree with Wilensky's conclusion that the moonlighter "is a man caught in a life-cycle squeeze—he has many dependents." [39] But this pattern obviously doesn't apply to hustlers—nor, for that matter, to the aforesaid typists and shopgirls who moonlight in prostitution.

(3) The external world. We saw that changes in American sporting life over the past three decades have severely damaged the hustler's work situation and career. These changes have reduced the number of places he can hustle in, the time-span in which he can stay unknown, the number of people he can hustle, and the average amount of money he can get from someone he hustles. Hustling is a dying trade.

Whenever an occupational group faces a disappearance or major decline of the market for its skills and a consequent inability to make ends meet, we conceptualize this situation as "technological unemployment." But this concept doesn't fit the situation of hustlers at all well. They suffer not from a shift in technology but from a shift in America's demographic structure, i.e., the decline of the bachelor subculture that populated poolrooms so heavily, and secondarily from a shift in fashion, i.e., the decline in the average amount of money bet on poolroom games. In origin, the hustler's problem is utterly unlike that of, say, the order clerk displaced by the introduction of electronic data processing. There is nothing whatever in the present technological structure of our society to prevent hustling (and poolroom life generally) from having or regaining its former place in America. It would seem, then, that occupational theory needs to complement the notion of "technological unemploy-

[39] Wilensky, *op. cit.,* p. 110.

ment" with notions such as "demographic unemployment" and "fashion unemployment."

A more general lesson of this essay is that sociology has unduly neglected the study of people who engage in sports or games for their livelihood. The sociological reason for this neglect is that sociology is compartmentalized into "fields" that tend to make such people, for all their visibility to the sociologist as citizen, invisible to him in his role as sociologist: such people are neglected by students of leisure because the latter are by definition concerned with sports involvement only in its impact on avocational life; and because sports involvement is for the very great majority of people strictly avocational, and those who earn a living at it constitute a minuscule fragment of the labor force, the study of the latter is neglected by occupational sociologists. Thus a largely unexplored area of social research consists of the people who work at what most of us play at.

Appendix: The Hustler and His Argot

Outsiders usually find a deviant group's argot to be one of the most interesting things about that group. But analysis of the argot requires an amount of space disproportionate to its importance in an over-all account of the group. To attenuate this conflict I have followed David Maurer's practice (in *The Big Con*) and relegated argot analysis to an appendix. Moreover, what follows is in no sense a full-scale study of hustlers' argot; it does not even contain a full vocabulary list. Instead, it examines the argot merely in its more sociological aspects—in its relation to hustling life and to the structural and functional features of argots in general.

A myth that dies very hard, even among linguists and social scientists, is that the special language or slang developed by a socially deviant group functions importantly to protect the group, has secrecy as a primary motive and mainspring. It dies hard because any outsider quickly notices on first acquaintance with such language that (a) it has terms for various shady processes and techniques, (b) it has terms to distinguish insiders from outsiders, and (c) he can easily be spotted as an outsider because he doesn't know, or misuses, some of the language. "Common sense" tells him that all this greatly aids group secrecy. But all it shows *eo ipso* is that the argot of any special group (deviant or otherwise) includes many terms for things peculiar to that type of group, is in good part a technical vocabulary that must be learned. The hustlers' argot is no exception.

Like all other American deviant argots I know of, it also reveals numerous facets that testify against a "secrecy" interpretation. Some examples: (1) Hustlers always use their argot among themselves when no outsiders are present, where it could not possibly have a secretive purpose. (2) The argot itself is not protected but is an "open secret," i.e., its meanings are quite easily learned by any outsider who wishes to learn them and is an alert listener or questioner. (3) The argot is elaborated far beyond any conceivable need to develop a set of terms for deviant phenomena, and even far beyond any need to develop a full-scale technical vocabulary (which subsumes the terms for deviant phenomena).

That last point indicates the true mainsprings of argot: in various specialized groups, be they deviant or merely specialized occupational groups, argots develop partly to provide a shorthand way of referring to technical processes but partly also as an elaborately inventive, ritualistic, often rather playful way of reinforcing group identity or "we-feeling." Thus the argot of hustlers sets them off not for the purpose of secrecy, but rather by way of helping their sense of colleagueship and *esprit de corps.*[40]

[40] Linguists commonly distinguish between two types of specialized slang: (a) a noncriminal group's specialized slang, called *argot,* which of course is unintelligible to outsiders (and thus may occasionally be used for secrecy), but nevertheless is developed and used primarily to meet the need for technical terms and secondarily as a way of bolstering group solidarity; and (b) a criminal group's specialized slang, called *cant,* which is designed and used primarily to make the group's conversation unintelligible to outsiders.

This distinction may have some validity when applied to the

Any secrecy function the argot serves is incidental, a bonus as it were, and hustlers certainly do not count on it. The hustler, like the members of secret societies discussed by Georg Simmel, knows that the only way to maintain group secrets is to keep his mouth shut about them in the presence of outsiders—not discuss them even in esoteric terms, which would, if anything, only make the outsider highly suspicious. For this reason hustlers actually use their argot much less when outsiders are present than when they are absent. To the very small extent that hustlers' collaborative swindling (dumping) requires some secretive communication in the presence of the swindled, such communication is, as we have seen, carried out not via argot at all but by a pre-arranged *ad hoc* signal ("the office") that is not standard argot and in fact is usually nonverbal.

The lexicon of hustler argot overlaps that of some other argots. First, there is considerable overlapping with general poolroom argot. I estimate that most regular poolroom players understand at least a third of hustler argot. (And since the portion they understand is not restricted to "innocent" technical terms but includes such items as "fish," this is further evidence against a secrecy function.) Hustler argot subsumes that of the poolroom world; it is poolroom argot plus about twice as many additions and elaborations. And, as one would expect from the fact that hustlers have a greater sense of collective identity than poolroom habitués in general, that portion of the argot under-

---

criminal speech of certain other countries in certain historical periods, but it is often uncritically assumed to hold good for American criminal speech also (see, for example, H. L. Mencken's *American Language,* 4th ed., p. 578). A lot of myth and nonsense about American criminals' so-called "cant" has been generated by linguists bookishly familiar with the history of specialized slang but unfamiliar with the actual lifeways of American criminals. I contend that "cant," in the linguists' sense of the term, has not been demonstrated to exist, and cannot be demonstrated to exist, for any American criminal group whatsoever.

An honorable exception among linguists is David Maurer. His discussion of the language of con men in his *The Big Con* (New York: Pocket Books, 1949, pp. 282–88) is, with one exception noted below, a model of sociological sense.

stood by non-hustlers isn't used by them with anywhere near the frequency that hustlers use it.[41]

Secondly, and quite understandably in view of the nature of hustling life, there is lexical admixture from other professional criminal argots, especially gamblers' argot. The most important such term is "action," used variously in the senses of "a bet" or "betting" or "an opportunity to bet" or "a situation involving betting." As the reader may have gathered by now, it is the most ubiquitous argot word in hustler speech. Some other criminal terms used by hustlers are: "the office"; "the wire" (in the phrase "to send" or "give" someone "the wire," to tip him off— not in the professional con man's sense); "score" (noun: an amount of money or goods won or taken; verb: to win or take money or goods); "mechanic"; "yard" ($100); "the joint" (jail), etc.

Finally, one should note—though it is technically part of general slang admixture rather than argot—that a huge dimension of the hustler lexicon is in the use of obscene exclamations ("motherfucker," "rat bastard," "cocksucker," *"chinga su madre,"* etc.). The hustler is particularly given to these exclamations when he unintentionally misses a shot. His use of such terms is far more frequent than one would expect simply from his lower-class origins. There are two reasons for this: (a) In general, obscenities are used oftener in the poolroom than elsewhere in lower-class life, because the main inhibition against their use (for all classes) is the presence of women—and the poolroom, like the army, is ordinarily an all-male institution. (b) The hustler spends more time than anyone else in this non-inhibiting milieu of the poolroom, and thus tends to develop

---

[41] A portion of poolroom argot, and consequently of hustler argot, is also used by that dwindling band of upper-class billiard players who play entirely or almost entirely in private men's clubs. For example, I find the hustler term "shortstop" (meaning an excellent player but of the second rank, one who can stop all but the top players) used in a billiard book issued by an upper-class club. [*Amateur Billiard Championship of America (Class A): A Souvenir.* . . . (New York: Knickerbocker Athletic Club, 1899), p. 18].

greater habitual use of obscenity than other poolroom players. For these reasons also, when a woman does enter an action poolroom it is the hustlers who are likely to feel most resentful, for they suffer the greatest inhibition of their characteristic mode of discourse.

An argot has a geography, which means not merely that it is used in various localities of a country but that typically its content varies a bit, at any given time, from one locality to another. Such variation takes two main forms: (a) The same thing may be referred to differently. Thus in one locality the usual criminal term for police may be "the Man," in another it may be "the fuzz," in another "the nabs," in another "busters," etc. (b) The same term may be used for different things. Thus the term "gunsel" among Illinois criminals means a homosexual who takes the female role, but among California criminals it means an armed robber. Both kinds of variation occur not only from one city to another, but in larger cities they sometimes occur from one neighborhood or friendship clique to another. Hustler argot seems unusually bare of such variations; the only significant exception is that one kind of hustling game is usually called "one pocket" in some cities and "pocket apiece" in others. The argot is strikingly uniform from one city to the next and, within large cities, from one poolroom to the next.

It is tempting to attribute this relative uniformity to intercity and inter-poolroom communication, to the fact that hustlers possibly move about oftener than members of most other argot-using groups. But intercity communication is not sufficient to deter the preservation of local linguistic patterns. (For example, many linguists once assumed that the rapid spread of radio ownership in the 1920's and 1930's would tend to level out American regional differences in pronunciation and semantic patterns, but the *Linguistic Atlas of the United States and Canada* abundantly disproved this assumption.) Rather, it seems attributable mostly to the hustler's strong traditionalism —something that will emerge more clearly when we look at the argot historically.

An argot varies in time as well as space. Over the years it adds and drops words; and some other words, though they remain in the argot throughout, have their meanings changed. (E.g., the criminal term "gunsel," some of whose current meanings are given above, once meant—among other things—an apprentice safecracker.) Such historical change is more rapid in argot than in the language at large (though less rapid than change in general slang); compendia of argot get out of date much sooner than a general dictionary does. Furthermore, the argots of socially deviant groups (e.g., drug addicts, jazz musicians, professional criminals) tend to change even more rapidly than argots of respectable trades; when an argot word of such a group gets to be common coin among outsiders, the insiders often replace it—again, not for purposes of secrecy, but by way of reaffirming their separateness and "in-groupness." (Thus, only outsiders these days still refer to a marihuana cigarette as a "reefer.") But despite these strong predisposing factors, the hustlers' argot shows hardly any evidence of historical change.

Of course the argot of pool and billiard hustlers didn't spring full-formed from Zeus's head; there must have been a developmental period in which words were added and others dropped. But this period, wherever it was, certainly antedated World War I. For as far back as I have been able to trace the argot of hustlers—about sixty years—it has been remarkably stable. During this entire time it seems that: (a) no new words have been introduced; (b) no words have become obsolete; (c) no words are obsolescent (used or understood only by old-timers); (d) only one word has become more generalized in its meaning; and (e) only three words have become more specialized in their meanings.

I believe this is related to the strong element of traditionalism in hustler ideology, to the fact that the hustler has more awareness of, involvement with, and reverence for his outstanding predecessors and their accomplishments than other kinds of deviants have for their historical counterparts—more than the usual professional criminal or drug addict; more, even, than the homosexual or jazz musician.[42] Certainly it is not due to any lack of linguistic inventiveness or playfulness on the hustler's part (as we shall see when we consider hustlers' nicknames).

A stigmatized group counter-stigmatizes by having at least one pejorative term for outsiders as a class. Outsiders (in this context think of all non-hustlers, in or out of the poolroom world) are likely to encounter this term at least as frequently as any other in the argot; that is why the term applied to outsiders by, for example, jazz musicians and many criminal groups, "squares," is now understood by nearly all outsiders and is indeed used by so many of them that it has ceased to be just an argot word and has become part of general American slang. A few argot words for outsiders, though, remain fairly esoteric, e.g., the homosexual term "jam." Hustler argot is unusual in that its term for outsiders, "suckers," is properly speaking not an argot word at all; that is, it did not originate with hustlers, or even in other deviant groups that use it, but was adopted from general American slang. This possibly may relate to the fact, noted earlier, that hustlers are unusually indifferent to the opinions of those who put them down, and hence would feel little need to develop counter-stigmatizing terms of their own.

Criminal or quasi-criminal groups commonly have a name for those outsiders considered to be prospects, for their actual or potential "victims." This is especially so for deviants who do their "victimizing" in a primary, face-to-face situation. Thus the con man has his "mark," the prostitute has her "john" or

---

[42] The homosexual's interest in famous predecessors tends to be limited to citing them for the purpose of self-justification. The jazz musician's interest in famous predecessors or their accomplishments tends to be limited to those few major breakthroughs of the recent past, such as the innovations of Charlie Parker, from which current developments are deemed to stem. (Jazz fans are often more involved with past history —much to the annoyance of the musician, who would prefer that his questioner stop bugging him to recall details of a recording date of 25 years ago and concentrate instead on current sounds.) The historical attitude of most pool and billiard hustlers is quite different; even teenage hustlers are often full of respectful and prideful lore about their forebears.

"trick," etc. But the hustler has no such special term. A few decades ago, when pool hustlers were also (and usually) called pool "sharks," their actual or potential victims were often called "fish." But for fifteen or twenty years now the term "shark" has not been used in this sense among hustlers themselves and among poolroom habitués generally (though it is still so used among older outsiders whose acquaintance with poolrooms ended years ago), and the term "fish" has been restricted to cover only a small minority of victims—those rare ones who keep returning for more beatings.[43] (The hustler's "fish" is thus comparable to the con man's "addict" rather than his "mark.") Today, hustlers use the term "sucker," which formerly had only one meaning (outsiders as a whole, i.e., all non-hustlers), indiscriminately to refer to (a) outsiders as a whole or (b) that particular class of outsiders who are actual or potential victims. Which of these meanings it has depends on the context, and in some contexts it can mean both at once (as in one hustler's remark to me, "The trouble today is that most of the suckers are wise.")

Perhaps the most striking aspect of the pool and billiard hustlers' argot is its development and use of nicknames. Well over half of all full-time hustlers have nicknames which they use regularly. My impression is that the percentage of them who have nicknames is not only higher than among either professionals or hustlers in other sports, but is higher than in any other adult group in America except for certain criminal groups (notably con men). A few hustlers acquired their nicknames in

[43] "Shark" survives in poolrooms with a specialized meaning as a transitive verb: to "shark" one's opponent means to upset or distract him while he's shooting, for example, by making a sudden movement in his line of sight when he is aiming. In addition to the specialization of "shark" and "fish," the word "hustler" itself has taken on a specialized meaning among hustlers. When they referred to themselves as "sharks" in the old sense, they often used "hustler" in the general slang sense of anyone who's alert and willing to take on any sort of odd job for a quick buck; now, of course, they use "hustler" in the narrower meaning of a member of their profession. For the early usages, and the period of overlap between the meanings of "shark" and "hustler," cf. Vogeler, *op. cit., passim.*

their pre-hustling childhood or adolescence—this is especially likely if the nickname refers to a physical characteristic of the hustler—but the good majority acquired such names after they entered hustling.

The following are the nicknames of some hustlers recently or currently active: Brooklyn Jimmy, Cornbread Red, Spanish Eddy, Sleepy, Blueshirt, Glendale Johnny, Fats, Wimpy, Harry the Russian, Snake, Whitey (three hustlers), Connecticut Johnny, Detroit Whitey, Brooklyn Johnny, Jersey Red, Blacky, Fifth Avenue Red, Miami, Shoes, Cicero, Gigolo, Subway, Country, Peter Rabbit, Weenie Beanie, Skinny Eddy, Squirrel, Fast Eddy,[44] Gypsy (two hustlers), Tallahassee, Boston Shorty, Rockaway Abe, Brooklyn Charlie, Johnny Irish, Big Gene, Charlie the Hat, the Knoxville Bear,[45] Derby, Dago Frankie, Lefty (three hustlers), Iron Joe, Bob the Destroyer, Jimmy Sure-Shot, Daddy Warbucks, and Tommy the Sailor.

Nicknames formed on similar principles were borne by hustlers active before 1920: Cowboy Weston, Boston Whitey, the Sicily Kid, Seattle Slim, Farmer Jones, Johnny Icewater, West Coast Willie, Dago Joe, Bowery Al.[46]

I had assumed at first that certainly this part of the argot, if no other, was used for purposes of secrecy or disguise. A nickname, I thought, would help a hustler to con because he, whose poolroom reputation is known via his nickname, could disguise his identity from the non-hustler by introducing himself by his real name (could con by "honestly" introducing himself). This hypothesis was completely disproven. The hustler doesn't keep his nickname from his opponent or anybody else in the poolroom; he is always pleased to use it and be referred to by it. For example: at the start of a game with a hustler I'd

---

[44] Fast Eddy was nicknamed after the character in the movie *The Hustler*—but ironically, for he exasperates opponents by shooting quite slowly.

[45] The Knoxville Bear is, however, more frequently referred to among hustlers by his real name, Eddy Taylor.

[46] These nicknames of pre-1920 hustlers are taken from Vogeler, *op. cit.,* p. 346.

seen but never met, I introduced myself by saying, "I'm Ned," and the hustler replied, "They call me Shoes." Most hustlers never use their real names (except occasionally with outsiders encountered outside the poolroom), not because these need to be hidden but simply because they prefer to be nicknamed. Like many other argot terms, these nicknames exist because, to quote the words of more than one hustler, "they lend a little color to the game."

This is to say that the hustler's nickname is a *monicker,* not an *alias.* True enough, the monicker of a hustler (or other criminal) may incidentally aid him when he is being sought by police, for the latter may be seeking him only under his real name whereas most of his colleagues and friends have never heard that name and know him only by his monicker. It is also true that hustlers sometimes have to dodge the police because of trouble over their criminal moonlighting jobs. But the hustler (or other criminal) trying to avoid arrest never depends on his monicker for this purpose; on the contrary, when on the lam and faced with any situation in which he must give his name— e.g., meeting new people, renting a room, buying a plane ticket —he uses neither his real name nor his monicker but temporarily adopts yet another name, a true alias.[47]

Though the chief reason for hustlers' use of monickers is, as indicated above, the furtherance of *esprit de corps,* additional factors bolster such use. Taken together, they probably account for the extremely high percentage of hustlers—old and young alike—with monickers. (a) Hustlers are overwhelmingly from the lower class, which makes more frequent use of nicknames in adulthood than other classes. (b) The hustlers' world overlaps other criminal circles that have high monicker rates (especially, other types of gamblers). (c) Hustlers are historically minded, and the use of monickers is one way of maintaining a long-standing craft tradition (the old-time hustlers also had

[47] Unfortunately David Maurer's discussion of monickers (*op. cit.,* p. 286), in failing to note the functional distinction between a monicker and an alias, misleadingly conflates the two.

monickers). (d) The monickers may also reflect a continuance of certain male-alliance aspects of adolescence. Relevant here is the fact that the poolroom world—at least the world of action rooms—is exclusively male, except on infrequent occasion.[48]

[48] After this book was in press one hustler, whose monicker is "Fats" and who alleges he is the model for "Minnesota Fats" in *The Hustler,* published a book of reminiscences: Minnesota Fats with Tom Fox, *The Bank Shot and Other Great Robberies* (Cleveland: World Publishing Company, 1966). Fats is a delightful storyteller, but his imagination and ego have resulted in a book that presents, along with much fact, much fiction as if it were fact.

3
Research Method, Morality, and Criminology

Experience with adult, unreformed, "serious" criminals in their natural environment—not only those undertaking felonies in a moonlighting way, such as pool hustlers, but career felons—has convinced me that if we are to make a major advance in our scientific understanding of criminal lifestyles, criminal subcultures, and their relation to the social system, we must undertake genuine field research on these people. I am also convinced that this research can be done by many more sociologists, and much more easily, than the criminology textbooks lead us to suppose.

No criminology textbook, on balance, encourages such field research; most criminology textbooks actively discourage it; no criminology textbook pays attention to techniques for solving problems connected with it; every criminology textbook to discuss it is concerned above all to offer copouts for avoiding it. This chapter tries to remedy such defects.

The reason for these defects is not far to seek. Field study of adult criminals requires among other things giving up, indeed carefully avoiding, any and every kind of social-work orientation; but in sociology's struggle to become a science it has been precisely criminology, of all the sub-fields of sociology, that has been least succesful in freeing itself from traditional social-work concerns.

In the years immediately ahead that struggle may be even more difficult, because of a recent retrograde development: lately a number of sociologists themselves have joined forces with social workers to promote extra-scientific goals in the name of science and have saddled us with new euphemisms for these goals, such as "applied sociology" and "action-oriented research." Some sociologists have come to this from mistaken

117

conceptions of science, others from being tired of being tired radicals, and others from an opportunistic appraisal of where most of the grant action is. Whatever the motive, they are wrong, and below I shall have to animadvert on their views insofar as these views affect criminology. But let us look first at the criminology textbooks.

I

Criminology textbooks can be roughly grouped in three basic categories, according to the means they employ to cop out.

The simplest technique, and in a way the most effective, is for the textbook writer to be so generally negligent and imprecise about research methods that no serious comparison or even description of different methods is offered, and consequently the troublesome question of whether field research might sometimes be the method of choice need never arise. This is the road taken, for example, in Marshall Clinard's *Sociology of Deviant Behavior*.[1] But it is atypical. The fact that statistics on crime in general, and on convictions in particular, are so obviously defective in so many ways—something no criminologist can avoid seeing and having to discuss—causes most textbook writers at least to break silence on this question.

A second mode of evasion, intellectually the shoddiest, illustrates the special kind of blindness that can sometimes be induced by a "labelling" stance.[2] It is represented at its ingenious best, or disingenuous worst, in the way Richard Korn and Lloyd McCorkle delimit the subject matter of their *Criminology and Penology:*

> Faced with evidence that large numbers of persons commit violations for which they are never prosecuted, we are led to the further conclusion that the *actual, objective*

[1] This is also true, despite its promising title, of the same author's "Research Frontiers in Criminology," *British Journal of Delinquency,* VII (October, 1956), pp. 110–22.
[2] For additional remarks on difficulties with the application of labelling theory, see Chapter 5.

extent of law breaking may, in itself, be an unreliable index of criminality. This conclusion is suggested by the recognition that criminality itself (as distinguished from law breaking) is a matter of social stigmatization and official action in the first place. . . . An act of actual law breaking does not become criminal in any realistic social or legal sense until and unless it is conventionally defined and officially acted upon.[3] [Italics in original.]

We need not deny the important consequences of either conventional definitions or official actions to see that the foregoing point of view is, first of all, a cover-up for the fact that most sociologists find it too difficult or distasteful to get near adult criminals except in jails or other anti-crime settings, such as the courts and probation and parole systems.

Secondly, and more importantly, it is an abdication of sociology's role as a special discipline able uniquely to discover knowledge and understandings of social life—abdication in favor of a misguided "democratic" notion that a society's official acts and conventional public definitions really tell us what the society is all about, and that the sociologist's main job is to count and codify them. The latter kind of operating definition of sociology, a very common one, produces nothing but hackwork, a flood of books whose conclusions are remarkable for little besides utter banality; which is why the intelligent layman so often decides that except for the statistics and the jargon, he has been a sociologist all his life and didn't know it.

If, on the other hand, sociology is what my teacher Louis Wirth used to claim it is, the study of how society is really run as distinguished from how the society's civics textbooks say it is

[3] Richard Korn and Lloyd McCorkle, *Criminology and Penology* (New York: Holt, Rinehart & Winston, 1959), p. 11.

Other texts using the Korn-McCorkle mode of copout sometimes do so via their definition of crime rather than of the criminal. Thus for Walter Reckless, the only "real" crimes are those that are officially recorded; see his *The Crime Problem* (New York: Appleton-Century-Crofts, 1961, 3rd ed.), pp. 23, 27. Still other criminology texts, such as the one by Ruth Cavan, dodge the issue by never coming to grips with the problem of definition at all. Some of these texts partake also of the first mode; in fact, Korn and McCorkle, when it comes to description and comparison of research methods, are fully as vague as Clinard.

run, then—Korn and McCorkle to the contrary—it is exactly
the discrepancies between law breaking and law enforcement
that comprise one of the most central topics of criminology. But
we are never going to know much about that topic, or many
another, until we get out of the jails and the courts and into the
field. Of course our ignorance can remain blissful if, like Korn
and McCorkle, we use labelling theory as a form of verbal
magic to convince ourselves that the only "real" criminal is a
caught criminal, one whom law enforcers have obligingly placed
where it is convenient for criminologists to study him.

II

Fortunately, most criminologists are not magicians, and the
typical criminology text is given rather early on to moaning
and groaning about the fact that criminals and the things they
do are not well represented by official crime statistics. (This
fact is then usually ignored in the later chapters.)

We still have much to learn on this matter of bias in official records. (Especially, when it comes to assessing historical
trends, I think we have much to learn from professional historians' techniques of weighing sources.[4]) But the better criminologists are trying hard. The trouble is that they are overly
grateful for small gains, and thus get trapped in halfway houses.
Two of these halfway houses are quite seductive.

One halfway house, whose foundations were firmly built by
Edwin Sutherland's work on white-collar crime, comprises research that ferrets out new information by looking beyond police and court statistics to the records of acts punished by other
governmental agencies of social control. Its definition of crime
includes *mala prohibita* as well as *mala in se,* which, lawyer-
sociologist Paul Tappan to the contrary, makes good juridical

---

[4] For a brilliant example of how a historian can dissect the biases
in official crime records and illuminate a good deal of social reality in
the process, see Margaret Gay Davies, *The Enforcement of English
Apprenticeship: A Study in Applied Mercantilism, 1563–1642* (Cambridge, Mass.: Harvard University Press, 1956), *passim.*

sense as well as good sociological sense.[5] Marshall Clinard's study of wartime pricing and rationing violations, *The Black Market,* is an excellent example of this kind of research. A recent offshoot of this Sutherland tradition is Mary Owen Cameron's study of shoplifters, *The Booster and the Snitch,* extraordinarily valuable because it uses, for the first time in criminology, data to be found in the records of private police (in her study, records of department-store detectives), which reveal many acts that are *mala in se* but nevertheless don't show up in official statistics.

A second halfway house consists essentially of using survey research methods to collect statistics on crime. The inchoate beginnings of this approach are in the special crime surveys undertaken by some states in the 1920's, but the modern scientific foundation was laid principally by James Short and F. Ivan Nye, who demonstrated that intelligently constructed anonymous questionnaires, intelligently distributed in schools, could be used to gather important and valid data on the distribution of delinquent acts among those who had not been adjudicated as delinquents.[6] Criminologists have been slow to develop possible variations of this method in the study of adult crime, and we don't really know to what degree it would work with adults. But it is an intriguing possibility to be explored.

[5] Paul Tappan's "Who is the Criminal?," *American Sociological Review,* XII (February, 1947), pp. 96–102, restricts crime to acts "adjudicated as such *by the courts*" (my italics) so as deliberately to exclude corporate violations of law, or of governmental directives issued under authority of law, that are adjudicated by non-court regulatory agencies of the state. Most jurists as well as social scientists, however, would agree with C. S. Kenny's *Outlines of Criminal Law* that crimes are simply "wrongs whose sanction is punitive and is in no way remissible by any private person," regardless of the type of enforcement machinery. Max Gluckman's *The Judicial Process Among the Barotse of Northern Rhodesia* (Glencoe, Ill.: The Free Press, 1955), from which I take Kenny's definition of crime, also notes approvingly (p. 346) Kenny's point that crimes are "tried by different procedures before various tribunals, and sanctioned in many degrees by various kinds of punishment and moral reprobation." On this view, Sutherland's "white collar crime" is most definitely crime.

[6] Cf. James F. Short, Jr., and F. Ivan Nye, "Reported Behavior as a Criterion of Deviant Behavior," *Social Problems,* 5 (Winter, 1957), pp. 207–213, and the references therein to other articles by these authors.

Halfway houses are of course better than the tents of reliance only on official crime statistics. It is also obvious that the number of criminologists is limited, that these halfway houses (and others) could have many rooms added to them, and that such construction work could keep every criminologist usefully busy for years. But this would hardly be the best allocation of manpower, because these are still *halfway* houses and we should also be constructing houses that take us all the way.

It is all very well to draw a fuller quantitative picture of the numbers and kinds of criminals or criminal acts. But we cannot use this to dodge what is the ultimate, qualitative task, particularly regarding career criminals whose importance to any theorist of human behavior, not to mention the rest of society, is so disproportionate to their numbers: providing well-rounded, contemporary, sociological descriptions and analyses of criminal lifestyles, subcultures, and their relation to larger social processes and structures.

That is just where criminology falls flat on its face. Especially in the study of adult career criminals, we overdepend on a skewed sample, studied in non-natural surroundings (anti-crime settings), providing mostly data recollected long after the event. Criminologists can tell you about Sutherland's Chic Conwell, but they can't give you comparable data on professionals of today, still less the many other kinds of data on professionalism in crime that Sutherland never got to at all; criminologists can tell you much (though by no means all) about the Capone mob or Luciano mob in the 1930's, but on organized crime today they are no better than Will Rogers (all they know is what they read in the newspapers) and are inferior to any good crime reporter (who knows a lot that can't be put in the newspapers). We are always going to be in this spot—always slowly fitting together a jigsaw puzzle that is decades out of date, and never even knowing if we have all the pieces, or the right pieces—unless we change our research methods.

This means—there is no getting away from it—the study of career criminals *au naturel,* in the field, the study of such criminals as they normally go about their work and play, the study ot "uncaught" criminals and the study of others who in the past have been caught but are *not* caught at the time you study them. We know how much valuable knowledge and insight has been gained from field study of all sorts of other people. We even know it in the case of juvenile delinquents, and even in the case of mildly criminal adults engaged in "victimless" crime, such as drug users, homosexuals, and prostitutes. There isn't the slightest reason to suppose that adult felons are an exception.

We know too, or ought to know by now, that data gathered from caught criminals, for reasons in addition to and quite apart from possible sampling bias, are not only very partial but partially suspect. These are data that are much too heavily retrospective; data from people who aren't really free to put you down; data often involving the kind of "cooperativeness" in which you get told what the criminal thinks you want to hear so you will get off his back or maybe do him some good with the judge or parole board; data from someone who is not behaving as he normally would in his normal life-situations; and, above all, data that you cannot supplement with, or interpret in the light of, your own direct observation of the criminal's natural behavior in his natural environment.

To put the argument another way: Animal behavior has a narrower range of determinants than human behavior, is much less complex and variable. And yet, in recent years, animal ecologists have demonstrated that when you undertake "free-ranging" study of an animal in his natural habitat, you discover important things about him that are simply not discoverable when he is behind bars.[7] Obviously we can no longer afford the convenient fiction that in studying criminals in their natural habitat, we would discover nothing really important that could not be discovered from criminals behind bars. What is true for studying the gorilla of zoology is likely to be even truer for studying the gorilla of criminology.

[7] Cf. George B. Schaller, *The Mountain Gorilla: Ecology and Behavior* (Chicago: University of Chicago Press, 1963); Irven DeVore (Ed.), *Primate Behavior: Field Studies of Monkeys and Apes* (New York: Holt, Rinehart & Winston, 1965).

III

And so we come to the third kind of copout to be found in the criminology texts, one that is fairly intelligent on this matter of field research: it grants the potential value of such studies, regrets the lack of them, and then proceeds, sadly but firmly, to give sophisticated rationalizations as to why nothing much can be done about this unfortunate lack. Here the leading text, as in so much else concerning criminology, is by Edwin Sutherland and Donald Cressey.

The main obstacle to studying criminals in the field, according to Sutherland and Cressey, lies in the fact that the researcher "must associate with them as one of them." Few researchers "could acquire the techniques to pass as criminals," and moreover "it would be necessary to engage in crime with the others if they retained a position once secured." [8] Where Sutherland and Cressey got this alleged fact they don't say and I can't imagine. It is just not true. On the contrary, in doing field research on criminals you damned well better *not* pretend to be "one of them," because they will test this claim out and one of two things will happen: either you will, as Sutherland and Cressey indicate, get sucked into "participant" observation of the sort you would rather not undertake, or you will be exposed, with still greater negative consequences. You must let the criminals know who you are; and if it is done properly (more on this below), it does not sabotage the research.

Another mistaken Sutherland-Cressey claim about field research on career criminals is that "few of them [criminals] would permit interrogations regarding their earlier lives or would volunteer information regarding the processes by which they became criminals." [9] A few won't but most will—they will, that is, if you aren't pretending to be "one of them." Some examples: A syndicate criminal connected with illegal control

---

[8] Edwin Sutherland and Donald Cressey, *Principles of Criminology,* 6th ed. (Philadelphia: J. B. Lippincott, 1960), p. 69.
[9] *Ibid.,* p. 69.

of bars and nightclubs has described to me how he entered his line of work. (The process was in all essential respects comparable to an upper-class youth "going into daddy's business.") A long-time professional burglar has described to me his teenage apprenticeship to an older burglar. (The apprenticeship took place with his father's knowledge and consent, the father's chief concerns being that the older burglar not make a punk out of his son and that he teach him how to stay out of jail.) A man in charge of a numbers operation grossing millions each year has described to me his entire career from the time he became completely self-supporting at the age of 12. It might also be noted that two of the aforementioned people have never been convicted of anything, and the third, over a career of more than twenty rather active years, has done less than three years' time.

Although criminologists need not "acquire the techniques to pass as criminals," there is another matter of individual competence that excludes, or rather should exclude, a number of would-be researchers; but it narrows the field in only limited degree. The problem, which criminology texts ought to talk about but don't, inheres in that requirement of telling criminals who you are. In field investigating, before you can tell a criminal who you are and make it stick, you have to know this yourself, know where you draw the line between you and him. If you aren't sure, the criminal may make it his business to see that you get plenty shook up, really rack you up about it. I shall come back to this matter later. My point here is that field research on criminals, to judge from reactions to my classroom pitch about the need for it, seems especially attractive to people who are still trying to find out who they are. I have had to learn to discourage converts who are going through various identity crises, and to indicate bluntly that for them field research on criminals is a good thing to stay away from. Unfortunately, it is often the people best able to overcome moralism and achieve genuine empathy with criminals who are most vulnerable to allowing empathy to pass into identity.

But that "screening" problem aside, most criminologists can

intelligently, safely, and successfully undertake field study of adult criminals if they put their minds to it. In what follows I shall discuss problems connected with this research method and techniques I have found useful for solving them; illustrate some gains in knowledge that can be made by means of this method; and counter some additional objections to this kind of research.

IV

Most difficulties that one meets and solves in doing field research on criminals are simply the difficulties one meets and solves in doing field research. The basic problem many sociologists would face in field work on criminals, therefore, is an inability to do field work. I cannot try to solve that problem here, but shall briefly indicate what I think is its nature before discussing problems peculiar to research on criminals.

Successful field research depends on the investigator's trained abilities to look at people, listen to them, think and feel with them, talk with them rather than at them. It does *not* depend fundamentally on some impersonal apparatus, such as a camera or tape recorder or questionnaire, that is interposed between the investigator and the investigated. Robert E. Park's concern that the sociologist become first of all a good reporter meant not that the sociologist rely on gadgets to see, hear, talk, and remember for him; quite the contrary, it asked the sociologist to train such human capacities in himself to their utmost and use them to their utmost in direct observation of people he wants to learn something about. But the problem for many a sociologist today—the result of curricula containing as much scientism as science—is that these capacities, far from being trained in him, have been trained out of him. He "knows" that Park-style sociology produced merely "reportage" (this is less than a half-truth at best) and insists that the real way for him to learn about people is to place one or more screens between him and them. He can't see people any more, except through punched cards and one-way mirrors. He can't talk with people any more, only "survey" them. Often he can't even talk *about* people any more, only about "data."

Colleagues in older disciplines have begun to give up such scientism—for example, psychologists studying child development have lately come out of the laboratory in droves to look at the child in his natural habitat—and when sociology has finished anxiously proving it is scientific it too will abandon scientism.

In what follows I shall take this problem of trained incapacity for field work as already solved. This means I shall assume, at the outset, that the sociologist is not a man who needs an NIMH grant to find a criminal, that he can humanly relate to non-sociologist humans and by asking around can quickly get introduced to a criminal or at least find out where one or more can be met.

But suppose he finds, say, a tavern where a jewel thief or loan shark or fence hangs out, and has him pointed out or is even introduced. What then? The problems have just begun.

One problem arises from the fact that a criminal judges the judges, puts down the people who put him down. Any representative of the square world initially encounters some covert if not overt suspicion or hostility; it is best to assume such feelings are there (in the criminal) even if they don't show, and that you are not going to get far unless and until you overcome those feelings. This problem, although it exists in studying a criminal enmeshed with the law, is usually magnified in dealing with an uncaught criminal in his natural surroundings, for the following reasons: (1) You are more of an intruder. As far as he is often concerned, it's bad enough that he has to put up with questioning when in the hands of the law, and worse when squares won't even leave him in peace in his own tavern. (2) He is freer to put you down and you are more on your own; you have no authority (police, warden, judge, parole board) to back you up. (3) There is more of a possibility that he might be hurt by you, that is, he has more to lose than someone already in jail. Going for you, on the other hand, is the fact that because you are not working in a law-enforcement setting you

might *possibly* be all right; and the sooner you firmly establish
in his mind that you are not any kind of cop or social worker,
the sooner that fact begins going for you.

The following paragraphs will not solve for every researcher
these and related problems, but will give some procedures—in
no special order—that I have found useful to overcome such
problems and often to prevent them from arising in the first
place. They should be understood as a first attempt to state
formally what I have arrived at on a more or less intuitive and
trial-and-error basis in dealing with uncaught criminals. They
might not work for every researcher, but I think they would
work for most.

1. Although you can't help but contaminate the criminal's
environment in some degree by your presence, such contamination can be minimized if, for one thing, you use no gadgets
(no tape recorder, questionnaire form) and, for another, do not
take any notes in the criminal's presence. It is quite feasible to
train yourself to remember details of action and speech long
enough to write them up fully and accurately after you get home
at the end of the day (or night, more typically). Historians accept an eyewitness account written immediately after the event
as decent evidence, even when by an untrained observer, and
there is no good reason to deny validity to similar accounts by
trained observers.

2. Most important when hanging around criminals—what I
regard as the absolute "first rule" of field research on them—is
this: initially, keep your eyes and ears open *but keep your
mouth shut*. At first try to ask no questions whatsoever. Before
you can ask questions, or even speak much at all other than
when spoken to, you should get the "feel" of their world by extensive and attentive listening—get some sense of what pleases
them and what bugs them, some sense of their frame of reference, and some sense of *their* sense of language (not only their
special argot, as is often mistakenly assumed, but also how they
use ordinary language). Even after all this has been learned, if
the researcher is a compulsive talker or otherwise longwinded,
if he can't shut up for considerable periods, he will be seriously

handicapped; his sheer verbosity, even if in "correct" language, will bother most informants (as it will lower-class people generally).

Until the criminal's frame of reference and language have been learned, the investigator is in danger of coming on either too square or too hip (anxiously overusing or misusing the argot). The result of failure to avert such dangers is that he will be put on or, more likely, put down, and end by provoking the hostility of his informant. True, sometimes a skillful interviewer can deliberately provoke hostility to good effect. But that technique is difficult except after long experience with the particular type of deviant one is studying; and in any case, outside of anti-crime settings it should be tried, if at all, only with milder kinds of deviants.[10]

3. Once you know the special language, there is a sense in which you should try to forget it. You cannot accurately assess any aspect of a deviant's lifestyle or subculture through his argot alone, although many investigators mistakenly try. Such attempts result in many errors, because there is often a good deal of cultural lag between the argot and the reality.

One cannot, for instance, assume that every important role in a deviant subculture is represented by a special term. An example: A distinctive role in the male homosexual subculture is played by that type of woman, not overtly lesbian, who likes to pal around with male homosexuals and often serves as a front for them in the heterosexual world; but although this role has, according to older homosexuals I know, existed for decades, it is only within the past several years that homosexual argot has developed a special term ("faghag") to refer to such a woman.

Conversely, the widespread use of a term for a deviant role is not always a good clue to the prevalence or even the existence of role incumbents. An example: In the American kinship system, the three basic types of incest are brother-sister, father-daughter, and mother-son. We have a common term, originating

---

[10] For a hilarious, but genuine, verbatim transcript of an interview in which the deviant's hostility is deliberately and usefully provoked by the interviewer, cf. "Terry Southern Interviews a Faggot Male Nurse," *The Realist*, No. 43 (September, 1963), pp. 14–16.

in Negro subcultures and now part of general American slang, to designate one partner in the third type ("motherfucker"), and no special terms for the other types. But the facts of American incest are the reverse of what the language might lead one to believe: brother-sister and father-daughter incest are frequent, whereas mother-son incest is so extraordinarily rare that the staff of the Institute for Sex Research, when I queried them about this a few years ago, had found only one case that they regarded as genuine.

Thus the presence or absence of special language referring to deviance is conclusive evidence for nothing except the presence or absence of such special language. It may sensitize you as to what to look for in actual behavior, but the degree of congruence between the language and the reality of deviance is an empirical matter to be investigated in each case.

Also, the researcher should forget about imputing beliefs, feelings, or motives (conscious or otherwise) to deviants on the basis of the origins of words in their argot. Whether the etymologies are genuine or fancied (what linguists call "folk" or "false" etymologies), they tell us nothing about the psychic state of the users of the words. One form of analysis, a kind of parlor version of psychoanalysis, implicitly denies this. I have seen it seriously argued, for example, that heroin addicts must unconsciously feel guilty about their habit because they refer to heroin by such terms as "shit," "junk," and "garbage." Actually, the use of any such term by a heroin addict indicates, in itself, nothing whatever about his guilt feelings or the lack thereof, but merely that he is using the term for heroin traditional in his group.

At best, deviant argot is supporting evidence for behavioral phenomena that the investigator has to pin down with other kinds of data.

4. It is easier, usually, to get acquainted first with criminals at their play rather than at their work. Exactly where this is depends on your individual play interests. Of course, initiating such contact means recognizing that criminals are not a species utterly different from you; it means recognizing not only that

there but for the grace of God (or whoever else you think runs the show) goes you, but that you do have some leisure interests in common with criminals.

In fact, one excellent way of establishing contact involves a small bit of fakery at the beginning, in that you can get to know a criminal on the basis of common leisure pursuits and *then* let him know of your research interest in him. (But this latter should be done quite soon, after the first meeting or two.) Where and how you start depends, other things being equal, on what you do best that criminals are also likely to be interested in. For example, in trying to make contact with criminals in a neighborhood new to me, I of course find it best to start out in the local poolroom. But if you can drink most people under the table, are a convivial barroom companion, etc., then you should start out in a tavern. If you know horses, start out at a horse parlor. If you know cards, ask around about a good poker game. If you know fighters, start out at the local fight gym.

5. If you establish acquaintance with a criminal on some basis of common interest, then, just as soon as possible, let him know of the differences between you if he hasn't guessed them already; that is, let him know what you do for a living and let him know why, apart from your interest in, say, poker, you are on his scene. This isn't as ticklish as it seems to people who haven't tried it—partly because of that common interest and partly because the criminal often sees, or can easily be made to see, that there may be something in it for him. For example, he may have some complaint about the outside world's mistaken view of him that you, as someone who has something in common with him, might sympathetically understand and correctly report. (Sometimes these complaints are in fact accurate—as, say, when a pimp complains that, contrary to public impression, his girls drum up their own business.) Or he may want to justify what he does. (For example, a numbers operator justified his activity to me on the basis of a localistic sort of patriotism; he feels that he, like local bookies, benefits local businessmen because when a player wins he spends some money with a neighborhood merchant before blowing the rest in further gam-

bling, whereas racetracks merely drain money out of the neighborhood and in fact out of the city.) Or he may be motivated by pride and status considerations, e.g., want to let you know that his kind of criminality is superior to other kinds. (Examples: A burglar tells me his line of work is best because "If you do it right, there are no witnesses." Another, indicating his superiority to pimps, told me that among his colleagues a common saying about a girl supporting a pimp is that "Maybe she'll get lucky and marry a thief." And a robber, indicating his scorn of con men, proudly informed me of one of his scores that "I didn't *talk* him out of it—I *took* it off him.")

These and similar motives are present not far below the surface in most criminals, and are discoverable and usable by any investigator alert for them.

6. In studying a criminal it is important to realize that he will be studying you, and to let him study you. Don't evade or shut off any questions he might have about your personal life, even if these questions are designed to "take you down," for example, designed to force you to admit that you too have knowingly violated the law. He has got to define you satisfactorily to himself if you are to get anywhere, and answering his questions frankly helps this process along.

Sometimes his definitions are not what you might expect. (One that pleased but also disconcerted me: "You mean they pay you to run with guys like me? That's a pretty good racket.") The "satisfactory" definition, however, is usually fairly standardized—one reason being that you are not the first noncriminal he's met who didn't put him down and consequently he has one or more stereotyped exceptions to his usual definitions of squares. And with a bit of experience you can angle for this and get yourself defined as, for example, "a square who won't blow the whistle" or "a square who likes to play with characters" or "a right square."

One type of definition you should always be prepared for (though it is by no means always overtly forthcoming) is the informant's assumption that you want to be like him but don't have the nerve and/or are getting your kicks vicariously. Thus one of the better-known researchers on drug addiction has been described to me by junkies as "a vicarious junkie," criminals often define interested outsiders as "too scared to steal," and so on. This type of definition can shake you if there is any truth in it, but it shouldn't; and indeed you can even capitalize on it by admitting it in a backhanded sort of way, i.e., by not seriously disputing it.

7. You must draw the line, to yourself and to the criminal. Precisely where to draw it is a moral decision that each researcher must make for himself in each research situation. (It is also to some extent a decision about personal safety, but this element is highly exaggerated in the thinking of those who haven't done field work with criminals.) You need to decide beforehand, as much as possible, where you wish to draw the line, because it is wise to make your position on this known to informants rather early in the game. For example, although I am willing to be told about anything and everything, and to witness many kinds of illegal acts, when necessary I make it clear that there are some such acts I prefer not to witness. (With two exceptions I have had this preference respected.) To the extent that I am unwilling to witness such acts, my personal moral code of course compromises my scientific role—but not, I think, irreparably.

8. There is another kind of compromise that must be made, this by way of keeping faith with informants. As the careful reader of some other parts of this book will gather, in reporting one's research it is sometimes necessary to write of certain things more vaguely and skimpily than one would prefer. But that is more of a literary than a scientific compromise; there need be no distortion of the *sociological* points involved.

9. Letting criminals know where you draw the line of course depends on knowing this yourself. If you aren't sure, the criminal may capitalize on the fact to maneuver you into an accomplice role.

The possibility of such an attempt increases directly as his trust of you increases. For example, I knew I was really getting somewhere with one criminal when he hopefully explained to me why I would make a fine "steerhorse" (which in his argot means someone who fingers a big score for a share of it). To receive such indication of "acceptance" is of course flattering— and is meant to be—but the investigator must be prepared to resist it or the results can be far more serious than anything he anticipates at the beginning of his research. I have heard of one social worker with violent gangs who was so insecure, so unable to "draw the line" for fear of being put down, that he got flattered into holding and hiding guns that had been used in murders.

10. Although I have insisted that in studying criminals you mustn't be a "spy," mustn't pretend to be "one of them," it is equally important that you don't stick out like a sore thumb in the criminal's natural habitat. You must blend in with the human scenery so that you don't chill the scene. One consequence is that often you must modify your usual dress as well as your usual speech. In other words, you must walk a tightrope between "openness" on the one hand and "disguise" on the other, whose balancing point is determined anew in each investigation. Let me illustrate this with an example.

During the summer of 1960, in the course of the research reported on in the next chapter, I spent much time with people involved in heroin use and distribution, in their natural habitats: on rooftops, in apartments, in tenement hallways, on stoops, in the streets, in automobiles, in parks and taverns. (The way I wrote up my material at the time—which I have not changed for its republication in this book—is an example of what I mean about keeping faith with informants.) On the one hand, I did not dress as I usually do (suit, shirt, and tie), because that way of dressing in the world which I was investigating would have made it impossible for many informants to talk with me, e.g., would have made them worry about being seen with me because others might assume I represented the law. But on the other hand, I took care always to wear a short-sleeved shirt or T-shirt and an expensive wristwatch, both of which let any newcomer who walked up know immediately that I was not a junkie.

11. A final rule is to have few unbreakable rules. Although the field investigator can, to a large extent, plan his dress, speech, and other behavior beforehand so as to minimize contamination of the environment he is investigating, such plans should be seen as provisional and subject to instant revision according to the requirements of any particular situation. Sometimes one also must confront unanticipated and ambiguous situations for which one has no clear behavioral plan at all, and abide the maxim *On s'engage et puis on voit.*

So much for the abecedarium I have evolved in studying criminals outside of jails. Obviously it is not exhaustive. But I hope it will encourage other sociologists to study adult criminals in their natural settings. A bit more needs to be said, however, about what the criminal's "natural setting" actually means.

Studying a criminal in his natural setting means not only studying him outside of any law-enforcement context. It means studying him in *his* usual environments rather than yours, in his living quarters or streets or taverns or wherever, not in your home or your office or your laboratory. And it means you mustn't "schedule" him, mustn't try to influence his shifting choices among his environments or interfere with his desire either for mobility or immobility. If he wants to sit in front of his TV set and drink beer and watch a ballgame for a couple of hours, so do you; if he wants to walk the streets or go bar-hopping, so do you; if he wants to go to the racetrack, so do you; if he indicates (for whatever reason) that it's time for you to get lost, you get lost.

Involved in all this is much more than making him feel comfortable and establishing "good rapport" (although that is of course important). Such free-ranging study, as the animal ecologists call it, is concerned to avoid as far as possible any serious disruption of his daily routine. (It will often thoroughly disrupt *your* daily routine; that's one of the unavoidable prices of this research method.) It thus provides a fluid research situation consisting of a series of *natural* events in the life of your subject (for example, his running into friends), which (1) allows you to make observations about his lifestyle you ordinarily wouldn't make, (2) causes you to think of important questions about him that ordinarily you wouldn't think of, (3) causes him to think of relevant things to tell you that he otherwise wouldn't think of, and (4) causes him to make explanations of certain events to you that he ordinarily wouldn't make.

Given the known results of comparable field research on animals and on humans, and given the known and suspected qualitative as well as quantitative defects of research on people in jails, there is every reason to hope that field study of career criminals would bring us much in the way of genuine additions to knowledge. Just how much remains to be seen. In the meantime, let us look at one small example concerning professionalism in crime.

V

As a result of getting to know a professional heavy man in his own environment I was able to observe quite naturally, and quite naturally remark upon, the fact that his revolver seemed unusual. (It was a .38 that had been remounted on a .44 frame.) This so pleased him that he not only explained the gun's origin but, with very little additional prodding on my part, I was able to elicit from him the following attitudes concerning this tool of his trade. (For the sake of brevity I run his remarks together by omitting my responses to them.)

> The only pistol you can count on is a revolver. Every real character [criminal] knows that. So do the cops. Did you ever see a cop with an automatic? When you read about a job where an automatic was involved, you know the guy was an amateur. Sometimes an automatic won't go off. Yeah, not very often, but it happens. Once is all you need. When you pull that trigger your life depends on it. You can't take that chance. You don't have that worry with a revolver. And a revolver is balanced better. You can be more accurate with it.
> Another thing, when you read about guys using .45's and such. That's just amateur stuff. You're giving up accuracy for a lot of power you don't need. Sure, maybe

it makes sense for an FBI man to use a .357 Magnum sometimes, 'cause sometimes he has to knock down a door and things like that. For me a .38 is plenty. But you can't go much lower. A .32 is the bottom. You want a gun that if you have to shoot somebody, he goes down. Take a .25; that's a gun that's fit for nothing but a lady's purse.

Most times what you're supposed to do is just throw down on somebody [point the gun at him]. You don't really use that pistol if you don't have to. That's show-off stuff too. And when you use it you don't shoot if you don't have to. You have to fade enough heat without maybe killing somebody, so what you do is you try to slap somebody 'cross the head with it. That's another reason for a revolver. You slap somebody 'cross the head with an automatic, that mechanism gets loose and starts rattling, and maybe it jams next time.

Possibly the same information might have been elicited from someone sitting in jail, but what evidence we have indicates otherwise. I am scarcely the first criminologist to have talked with such a criminal, and moreover I am not an especially skillful interviewer, yet this kind of information cannot be found in previous criminological literature (at least, after much searching I cannot find anything like it). Why not? The most reasonable conclusion is that the novelty of the data derives from the novelty of the situation, from the free-flowing sequence of natural events in the criminal's life within which my observations and verbalizations were embedded and within which they could reinforce each other.

The remarks of a professional heavy man quoted above perhaps typify the attitude of such a craftsman toward the tools of his trade, and perhaps they do not. We don't know. That is in fact my complaint: we just don't know, and we will never know unless criminologists bestir themselves to do field studies of a good number of such criminals.

Given a cumulation of field researches, however, we would scientifically "know" a great deal more than we do now. That brings me to another copout concerning field study, which is succinctly formulated by Sutherland-Cressey and garbled in some other texts (for example, Taft and England): "One individual could not build upon the work of another to a very great extent, for precise, controlled techniques of observation could scarcely be employed." [11]

In countering this view I note, firstly, that providing "precise, controlled techniques of observation" which can be exactly duplicated by other investigators is a problem hardly unique to field research. It is just as much of a problem in the study of criminals who are seen in jail, or in the office of a parole officer, or in one's own office, or even in the experimental laboratory. And if this criticism applies to field research, it applies *a fortiori* to the cumulation of knowledge by means of retrospective autobiographical data such as form the basis of Sutherland's *The Professional Thief*.

Secondly, to make an absolute fetish of "precise, controlled techniques of observation" is to put the cart before the horse. It often is, in the jargon of sociology, a dysfunction of the bureaucratizing of our profession, the converting of a means into an end in itself so that the attainment of the original end is subverted. That is why some non-sociologist investigators of crime who know nothing of this fetish, such as the English teacher David Maurer in his *The Big Con* and the newspapermen Ed Reid and Ovid Demaris in their *The Green Felt Jungle*, have, for all their sloppiness and naiveté from a sociologist's point of view, produced valuable studies of career crime that put the criminologist to shame. (Rather, such books ought to make the criminologist feel ashamed of himself, but unfortunately they don't.)

Thirdly, to impose on the field worker some of the controls that purists want—to insist that different field researchers studying, say, loan sharks, must each ask their subjects exactly the same questions in exactly the same order in exactly the same words (or worse yet, insist that the subjects must fill out questionnaires or talk into a tape machine or that the researcher take notes in their presence)—is severely to contaminate the very thing we want to study, the reactions of people *in their natural environment*. Sociology isn't worth much if it is not

[11] Sutherland and Cressey, *op. cit.*, p. 69.

ultimately about real live people in their ordinary life-situations, yet many of the "precise, controlled techniques of observation" introduced by the investigator produce what is for the subject anything but an ordinary life-situation.

Fourthly, for all the variety of "natural environments" in which different investigators of loan sharks would find themselves, and thus the necessary *and desirable* differences in investigators' procedures (when to ask questions and when to shut up, what words to use, and so on), there would remain a large amount of comparability. Sutherland and Cressey notwithstanding, we could get knowledge of a genuinely cumulative kind, for example, an increasingly accurate notion of the typical pattern of loan sharks' relations with police. We might even one day arrive at the millennium: an accurate estimate of the size of the universe (all loan sharks) and the degree of representativeness of the sample, and be able to formulate that "typical pattern" in a way satisfying to the hardnosed statistician. But we will never come close if we never try.

In sum, the "scientific" objections to field research on criminals that one finds in Sutherland-Cressey and other texts are either no objections at all or apply to all sorts of other sociological research and boil down to the truism that our research methods in general fall short of perfection. The regularity with which criminologists focus on alleged scientific objections to field research, and the regularity with which they ignore or barely hint at the obvious *moral* objection to such research, suggests that the issue of morality is really what bothers them most. The moral issue deserves closer examination than the criminology textbooks give it.

VI

If one is effectively to study adult criminals in their natural settings, he must make the moral decision that in some ways he will break the law himself. He need not be a "participant" observer and commit the criminal acts under study, yet he has to

witness such acts or be taken into confidence about them and
not blow the whistle. That is, the investigator has to decide
that when necessary he will "obstruct justice" or have "guilty
knowledge" or be an "accessory" before or after the fact, in
the full legal sense of those terms. He will not be enabled to
discern some vital aspects of criminal lifestyles and subcultures
unless he (1) makes such a moral decision, (2) makes the
criminals believe him, and (3) convinces them of his ability
to act in accord with his decision. That third point can sometimes be neglected with juvenile delinquents, for they know that
a professional studying them is almost always exempt from
police pressure to inform; but adult criminals have no such
assurance, and hence are concerned to assess not merely the
investigator's intentions but his ability to remain a "stand-up
guy" under police questioning.[12]

To my knowledge, Lewis Yablonsky is the only criminologist who has had the good sense and emotional honesty to
object to such research primarily on moral grounds. He claims
that the views expressed in the foregoing paragraph (as originally published), and any similar views, go too far from a
moral standpoint. According to Yablonsky, nonmoralizing on
the part of the researcher, when coupled with intense interest
in the criminal's life, really constitutes a romantic encouragement of the criminal.[13]

Not so. To be sure, the research involvement I recommend
is hardly uninterested; but also obviously, it tries to be as far
as humanly possible *dis*interested, a scientific undertaking concerned neither to confirm the criminal in his criminality nor
to change him, but to understand him. Furthermore, if the
sociologist himself has any lingering "romantic" view of criminality, there is nothing so effective as close association with
criminals to get him over it, because criminals themselves—at

[12] The foregoing paragraph was originally published, in slightly different form, as a footnote I contributed to Howard Becker's *Outsiders*
(New York: The Free Press of Glencoe, 1963), p. 171.

[13] Lewis Yablonsky, "Experiences with the Criminal Community,"
in Alvin Gouldner and S. M. Miller (Eds.), *Applied Sociology* (New
York: The Free Press, 1965), p. 72.

least those who are beyond the novice stage and seriously committed to crime as a career—are usually quite hardheaded and unromantic about it all. In any case, the criminal scarcely needs the sociologist to make him feel important as an object of romantic interests when, every day, every TV set in the land blares forth such messages for those criminals interested in picking up on them.

It is possible—highly doubtful, but possible—that a few criminals might become more set in their criminality, to some minuscule degree, by the mere fact that my type of investigating is totally unconcerned to "reform" them or "rehabilitate" them or "make them see the error of their ways." But in the first place, such unconcern is qualitatively different from positive encouragement or approval. (Indeed, part of what I conceive to be proper research technique with criminals, as indicated previously, involves letting them know who you are and what you do for a living, which means letting them know that your value choices are different from theirs.) Secondly, the burden of proof rests upon those who claim that abstention from moralizing by the field investigator has any significantly encouraging effect on criminals' lifestyles, and they have not supplied one bit of such proof. Finally, our society at present seems plentifully supplied with moral uplifters in any case, so one needn't worry if a few sociological students of crime fail to join the chorus.

VII

And there are only a few such sociologists. Unfortunately, Yablonsky's outlook prevails among those sociologists who define themselves as criminologists. The great majority of criminologists are social scientists only up to a point—the point usually being the start of the second, "control of crime," half of the typical criminology course—and beyond that point they are really social workers in disguise or else correction officers *manqués*. For them a central task of criminology, often *the* central task, is to find more effective ways to reform law-breakers and to keep other people from becoming lawbreakers.[14]

If a man wants to make that sort of thing his lifework I have no objection; that is his privilege. I suggest merely that he not do so in the name of sociology, criminology, or any social science. I suggest that he admit he is undertaking such activity not as a social scientist but as a technologist or moral engineer for an extra-scientific end: making people obey current American criminal law. This is not to deny his right as an ordinary citizen to be "engaged" and make value judgments about crime, politics, sex, religion, or any other area of moral dispute. Rather, it is to deny that everything appropriate to one's role as ordinary citizen is appropriate to one's role as scientist, and to insist that making such value judgments is not only inappropriate to the latter role but highly inimical to it.

To locate such inimical effect one need look no further than Yablonsky's own admission that in his work with juvenile delinquents "some gang boys who met with me almost daily—some over several years—never fully believed that I was not 'really a cop.' "[15] Any student of deviance who confounds the

[14] An awareness that criminology is dominated by self-styled sociologists who are basically social workers perhaps lies behind the Columbia University sociology department's long refusal to harbor criminologists and its correlative banishment of them to the School of Social Work. Such awareness on Robert Merton's part, at least, would logically follow from his negative evaluation of his early "slum-encouraged provincialism of thinking that the primary subject-matter of sociology was centered in such peripheral problems of social life as divorce and juvenile delinquency." (See his "Introduction," *Social Theory and Social Structure* [Glencoe, Ill.: Free Press, 1949], p. 17.) The mistake made by Columbia's sociology department is that in throwing out criminology as a major sub-field it abandons a beautiful sociological baby to drown in all that social-work bathwater.

Given the perspectives within which delinquency and crime are almost always studied, it is obvious why Merton might regard them as "peripheral problems of social life" rather than fundamental social processes of central concern to sociology. But it is also obvious that, in every society, among the really fundamental social processes are those which involve transgression of the society's moral norms by some people and reaction by others to such transgression, and indeed that these processes bear crucially on the most fundamental sociological question of all, the question of how social order is possible.

[15] Lewis Yablonsky, in Gouldner and Miller, *op. cit.*, p. 56.

roles of social worker and sociologist ("the dual role of prac-
titioner-researcher," as Yablonsky puts it) is bound to elicit
that sort of response and have his research flawed by it. And
if failure to solve this problem is serious in the scientific study
of delinquents, failure to solve it in the study of adult career
criminals is catastrophic.

The failure derives from what is truly a romantic ideology,
one common to "applied sociologists": a sentimental refusal
to admit that the goals of sociological research and the goals of
social work are always distinct and often in conflict. The conflict happens to be extremely sharp in the case of adult felony
crime. The criminologist who refuses fully to recognize this
conflict and to resolve it *in favor of sociology* erects a major
barrier to the extension of scientific knowledge about such
crime and such criminals.

But what of one's duty as a citizen? Shouldn't that take
precedence? Well, different types of citizens have different
primary duties. And our very understanding of "citizenship"
itself is considerably furthered in the long run if one type of
citizen, the criminologist, conceives his primary duty to be the
advancement of scientific knowledge about crime even when
such advancement can be made only by "obstructing justice"
with respect to particular criminals in the short run.

Many an anthropologist has been able to advance the state
of knowledge only by keeping faith with people who radically
transgress the moral norms of his society, that is, by refusing
to turn them in to colonial officials and their cops, so I fail to
see why the criminologist shouldn't do the same. Of course,
if someone really wants to behave toward the savages as a
missionary rather than as an anthropologist, if he really wants
to be a superior sort of social worker or cop or therapist rather
than a sociologist, there is no denying him this right; but at
least let him own up to what he really is and stop fouling the
waters of science with muck about "the dual role of practitioner-
researcher."

I would not wish to be understood as claiming that the
criminologist, in his role as criminologist, must ignore value

judgments. On the contrary, he might scientifically deal with
them in several ways well known to sociology. For example,
he could study how a society came to have the particular
moral norms that it has, or study the unanticipated consequences of these norms for the society, or study the differential
distribution and varying intensity of these norms within different subcultures of a complex society. The sociologist or
criminologist can, as a scientist, do the foregoing things and
more with respect to values. But if some people claim that
whatever the law may say at the moment, it is "right" (or
"wrong") to do this or that and they act in accord with their
value judgment, one thing the sociologist or criminologist can
not do, directly or indirectly, is to gainsay them and interfere
with their lives in the name of his science. The social scientist
has no business attempting to "adjust" people to the moral
norms of his society or any other.

Max Weber, in emphasizing that sociology must be value-
neutral if it is to be genuinely scientific, long ago made the key
distinctions between one's role as ordinary citizen and one's role
as social scientist. Our allegedly sociological students of crime,
however, have forgotten Weber's lesson if, indeed, they ever
learned it.

It is hard to blame them when they see other social scientists directly criticize Weber's fastidiousness about value-neu-
trality out of a gluttonous desire to have their cake and eat it,
to be moralizers and scientists at once. But the criticism levelled
at Weber on this matter, whether by "natural law" ideologues
such as Leo Strauss or "applied sociology" ideologues such as
Alvin Gouldner, comes to no more than the statement that the
value-neutral ideal is impossible of full attainment and that
even the great Max Weber could not always keep his personal
values completely out of his scientific work. Such criticism is
quite true and equally irrelevant: although the ideal is indeed
not fully attainable, there are radically different degrees of
approximation to it that are attainable, and these quantitative
differences add up to a significant difference in quality; which is

to say that if we try like hell we can come very close to the ideal and enormously improve the state of our science thereby. But the critics of Weber aren't interested in trying. They apparently believe that because we cannot be virgin pure with respect to value-neutral social science we might as well be whores.

Actually, two related modes of sociological inquiry can prod us toward objectivity. One, indicated above, consciously excludes value judgments to a degree that comes close to the Weberian ideal, so much so that it can even produce findings which go against the personal values of the investigator. (For example, Chapter 5 reports conclusions about highly erotic art that seem to me inescapable as a sociologist but that I personally regret having to report—because they give ammunition to censors, whom I detest.) The related mode, suggested to me by Howard Becker and illustrated in Chapter 2, counterbalances the values of one's society—and the investigations by social workers or "applied sociologists" of one's society—by using an "anti-social" perspective, e.g., by viewing society as a "problem" for the deviant rather than the other way round. Although such counterbalancing need not be restricted to criminology—one could, for example, sympathetically study the racist's "problem" of how to check desegregation and increase racial discrimination—it is likely to have especially salutary effects there. This route to value neutrality I find adumbrated not in Max Weber's work but in Friedrich Nietzsche's *Genealogy of Morals:*

> It is no small discipline and preparation of the intellect on its road to final "objectivity" to see things for once through the wrong end of the telescope; and "objectivity" is not meant here to stand for "disinterested contemplation" (which is a rank absurdity) but for the ability to have the pros and cons in one's power and to switch them on and off, so as to get to know how to use, for the advancement of knowledge, the *difference* in the perspectives and psychological interpretations. . . . All seeing is essentially perspective, and so is all knowing. The more emotions we allow to speak on a given matter,

the more different eyes we train on the same thing, the
more complete will be our conception of it, the greater
our "objectivity."

VIII

My complaint, however, is basically Weberian in origin: I
object not that criminologists have an anti-criminal moral code
but that it is misplaced morality, acted upon within the scientific role instead of being kept firmly outside it. Such misplace-
ment is not only inappropriate to scientific endeavor but clearly
detrimental to it: I have tried to show that although criminologists sometimes give lip service to the scientific ideal of dis-
passionately studying criminals in the open, they immediately
subvert that ideal. Obviously they do so out of fear of being
caught with their anti-criminal values down. Their misplaced
morality leads them, in practice, to pass up the field study of
criminals, to invent various rationalizations for avoiding it, to
exaggerate its difficulties, and to neglect some fairly obvious
techniques for avoiding these difficulties.

But if the criminologist wants to help build a real science—
for example, if he wants to go beyond his ritualistic wailing
over the inadequacies of retrospective data and official statistics
and really do something about these inadequacies—he might
ponder the reaction of Bronislaw Malinowski, exactly forty years
ago, to a similar situation that then obtained in anthropology:

> We are obviously demanding a new method of collect-
> ing evidence. The anthropologist must relinquish his
> comfortable position in the long chair on the veranda
> of the missionary compound, Government station, or
> planter's bungalow, where, armed with pencil and note-
> book and at times with a whisky and soda, he has been
> accustomed to collect statements from informants, write
> down stories, and fill out sheets of paper with savage
> texts. He must go out into the villages, and see the
> natives at work in gardens, on the beach, in the jungle.
> ... Information must come to him full-flavored from his
> own observations of native life, and not be squeezed out
> of reluctant informants as a trickle of talk. Field work

can be done first or secondhand even among the savages, in the middle of pile dwellings, not far from actual cannibalism and head-hunting. Open-air anthropology, as opposed to hearsay note-taking, is hard work, but it is also great fun. Only such anthropology can give us the all-round vision of primitive man and primitive culture.[16]

Until the criminologist learns to suspend his personal distaste for the values and lifestyles of the untamed savages, until he goes out in the field to the cannibals and headhunters and observes them without trying either to civilize them or turn them over to colonial officials, he will be only a veranda anthropologist. That is, he will be only a jailhouse or courthouse sociologist, unable to produce anything like a genuinely scientific picture of crime.

IX

But if one refuses to be a sociologist of the jailhouse or court system, takes Malinowski to heart, and goes out into the field, there is risk involved. At least I have found this so in my own experience. It is the sort of risk that writers of criminology texts, for all their eagerness to put down field work, surprisingly don't mention; most of the danger for the field worker comes not from the cannibals and headhunters but from the colonial officials. The criminologist studying uncaught criminals in the open finds sooner or later that law enforcers try to put him on the spot—because, unless he is a complete fool, he uncovers information that law enforcers would like to know, and, even if he is very skillful, he cannot always keep law enforcers from suspecting that he has such information.

Although communication between someone and his wife or lawyer or doctor is legally privileged (these people cannot be required to divulge the communication), there is no such status accorded a communication between anyone and the

[16] Bronislaw Malinowski, *Myth in Primitive Psychology*, 1926; as republished in his *Magic, Science, and Religion* (New York: Doubleday Anchor Books, 1954), pp. 146–47.

criminologist. The doctrine of legally privileged communication has so far been extended only to cover certain of those other professionals (nurses, priests, psychotherapists) who are in a "treatment" relationship with clients. Possibly the social-worker sort of criminologist dedicated to "rehabilitating" criminals might find shelter under this legal umbrella, but the scientific criminologist presumably could not. If the latter criminologist stood fast on his obligation to protect informants in the face of law enforcers' demands that he tell all, the guiding judicial precedents most likely would be the cases of journalists who have done likewise in legally unprotected situations, and he would be held in contempt of court. I know of no instance where this has actually happened; but if a significant number of criminologists began doing the kind of research I recommend, we would probably get an instance soon.

On the other hand, few criminologists are soon likely to undertake serious field research on serious adult criminals. The odds are great that nearly all criminologists, even those not desiring to be social workers, will continue to complain about the defects of our data on crime and criminals but will also continue to duck the best way of overcoming these defects— some, perhaps, because they wish to avoid the contingency of being put on the spot by law enforcers, and most because of guilt feelings involved in obtaining information on felons and their felonies that one knows would be useful to law enforcers but does not report. If the very few of us concerned to do such field research are ever to convert most of our colleagues, we will have to abate their fears and ease their consciences a good bit more.

Either we will have to force and win a legal test case on this matter of research privilege for criminologists (I for one would be willing to be the guinea pig), or, in the more likely event that no judicial basis can be found for such a test case, we will have to obtain new statutes. Should we manage by either method to get the communication between criminal and criminologist accorded the same legal status as that between criminal and lawyer, then field research on adult criminals would really come into its own, for we would at once have provided the necessary stiffening of criminologists' spines and have removed the biggest single obstacle to cooperation from our research subjects.

However, I see no reason to be hopeful that we will be granted this legal privilege, and in fact am quite pessimistic. In the foreseeable future, field research on criminals will have to be carried out under the hazards and handicaps that now obtain. But even under present conditions such research can be done. And if we are serious about studying crime scientifically, it must be done.

4
The Village Beat
Scene: Summer 1960*

> Now, it is obviously easier to recognize ideologies wher-
> ever they are strongly institutionalized or highly verbal.
> . . . The true meaning of ideology for identity formation,
> however, can be fathomed only by descending into those
> transitory systems of conversion and aversion which
> exist in . . . adolescence. Such implicit ideologies are
> often overtly and totally unideological; yet they often
> exist as the most vital part of a young person's or
> group's life, as a basis for a tentative and yet total
> orientation in life, without the knowledge or, indeed,
> curiosity, of the adults around them.—*Erik Erikson* [1]

This essay is both more and less than a portrayal of the beats of
Greenwich Village and its environs. More, because much of it
holds good for beats elsewhere. Less, because I have not
depicted some of the Village beat world's well-publicized aspects, but have tried for completeness only in regard to the
changes that have taken place in that world since my last
acquaintance with it (1957). I use the word "beat" for brevity
and ask readers to note that it obscures as much as it
illuminates.

* This chapter originally appeared in *Dissent,* Vol. 8, No. 3 (Summer, 1961), pp. 339–59. I have added to the text and notes at several
points; these additions are indicated by brackets.
Readers interested in other of my views on this subject should consult: (a) my reply to Norman Mailer's "The White Negro" and his
rejoinder to me, *Dissent,* Vol. 5, No. 1 (Winter, 1958), pp. 77–81, both
of which are reprinted in Mailer's *Advertisements for Myself* (New
York: Putnam, 1959), pp. 365–71; (b) my debate with Irving Howe in
Partisan Review, Vol. 27, No. 2 (Spring, 1960), pp. 379–83.
[1] "Identity and Totality," in *Human Development Bulletin, Fifth
Annual Symposium* (Univ. of Chicago, 1954), p. 68. A full psychological analysis of the beats, which I do not attempt, should in general
proceed along Eriksonian lines. But in view of the significant minority
of beats in their thirties and forties, it should place greater stress on the
persistence in more or less chronic form of some psychic states charac-
terizing acute adolescent phenomena.

I

The individuals in question resent any label whatever, and regard a concern with labelling as basically square. But insofar as they speak of themselves generically and are forced to choose among evils, they prefer the word "beat." Until recently "hipster" meant simply one who is hip, roughly the equivalent of a beat. Beats recognized that the hipster is more of an "operator"—has a more consciously patterned lifestyle (such as a concern to dress well) and makes more frequent economic raids on the frontiers of the square world—but emphasized their social bonds with hipsters, such as their liking for drugs, for jazz music, and, above all, their common scorn for bourgeois career orientations. Among Village beats today, however, "hipster" usually has a pejorative connotation: one who is a mannered showoff regarding his hipness, who "comes on" too strongly in hiptalk, etc. In their own eyes, beats are hip but are definitely not hipsters.

Although beats are characteristically ignorant of history, even of their own history, most know the oft-discussed origin of "beat" as applied to the postwar disaffected. But all are in the dark about "hip." The few Village beats with any opinion suppose that it comes from the "hep" of early 1940's jivetalk. Actually "hep" and "hip" are doublets; both come directly from a much earlier phrase, "to be on the hip," to be a devotee of opium smoking—during which activity one lies on one's hip. The phrase is obsolete, the activity obsolescent.

As early as 1938 David Maurer noted that due to the rapid decline of opium smoking much of its argot was being loosely transferred to other types of drug taking, "frequently without a full knowledge of the original meanings of the words transferred." [2] Today's use of "hip" extends this process, for now

[2] Cf. Maurer's "Argot of the Underworld Narcotic Addict: Part II," *American Speech*, Vol. 13 (October, 1938), p. 179, fn. 3. Cf. also Alfred Lindesmith, *Opiate Addiction* (Bloomington, Indiana: Principia Press, 1947), p. 215.

the word has the generalized meaning of "in the know" and even among beat drug users doesn't always refer specifically to knowledge of drugs.

II

Paradoxically, nearly all articles on the beats neglect the thread that colors beat life: the overwhelming majority of beats are *not* exhibitionists or publicity-seekers but precisely the opposite. Articles by beat writers, who belong nearly always to the publicity-seeking minority, implicitly deny this fact. And square writers, who as often as not simply lift their material from beat writings, don't know this fact, or minimize it because it is unexciting, or explicitly deny it. One of the rare exceptions is Caroline Bird, who nearly four years ago correctly noted of the beat that "his main goal is to keep out of a society which, he thinks, is trying to make everyone over in its own image. . . . He may affect [distinctive dress] but *usually prefers to skulk unmarked*." [3] Today, despite the attention given to beats in the mass media, despite the consequence that some beats now resemble professional "angry young men" securing toeholds in the lower levels of our "establishment" (the slicker cheesecake magazines) and yearning for our peculiar version of the aristocratic embrace (*Life*), Miss Bird's observations are still generally valid.

Nearly all Village beats most of the time and most of them all of the time want not even a hostile relationship with squares. They restrict their relations with squares to that bare minimum needed to live at all. Many a beat, sociable enough with other beats, goes for weeks at a time without engaging in a single real conversation with a square, his "conversation" with squares being limited to the few ritualistic phrases required to make food purchases, etc. Moreover, the large majority of beats do not flaunt their physical presence before the public gaze. Most

[3] "Born 1930: The Unlost Generation," *Harper's Bazaar,* February 1957. My italics.

beats dress in an ordinary lower-class manner, distinctive only to middle-class eyes. A substantial minority, between a fourth and a third, also wear various kinds of badges (beards, typically) but usually do so as a ready means of identifying themselves to one another and to promote a "we" feeling, not out of a desire to call the attention of outsiders to themselves. Most of even this badge-wearing minority want to remain quite inconspicuous as far as squares are concerned. Their badges are meant for fellow beats, and were worn long before publicity made the squares aware of them; it will hardly do to call these beats "exhibitionists" just because squares have lately stolen their signals. These fundamental points are garbled or suppressed, when known at all, as more and more writers discover a market for articles on "colorful" beats.

It is indeed obvious to the tourist that some beats need frequently to proclaim their negative identities by costume and behavior designed to shock. But that is no reason for even our social scientists to remain merely tourists and write, for example, as if beats typically were devoted to "conspicuous consumption of the self"—an absurdity comparable to suggesting that most homosexuals are drag queens.[4] To describe only what is more or less deliberately exposed to tourist view is to forget that the cool world is an iceberg, mostly underwater.

III

There has been in three years a great proliferation of Village coffee shops, chiefly because square patronage makes them profitable. New York's beat scene has become a major tourist attraction, just as happened earlier in San Francisco.

___

[4] [The quoted phrase and related nonsense may be found in Ernest van den Haag's "Conspicuous Consumption of Self," *National Review,* Vol. VI, No. 23 (April 11, 1959), pp. 658–60. The phrase (and concept) appears to be an unacknowledged borrowing from Anatole Broyard's "A Portrait of the Hipster," *Partisan Review,* Vol. XV, No. 6 (June, 1948), p. 727; Broyard correctly applied it to the prototypical hipster of the early 1940's, whose lifestyle was in key respects different from that of the beats a decade later.]

[In the summer of 1960 the Village beat scene was at its very peak because, among other things, most of the San Francisco beats had by then become so harassed by tourist hordes and police that they fled to New York.[5] Shortly after this study was finished the same thing happened in Greenwich Village; the exodus of Village beats to the lower East Side—already begun at the time of my study—entered full swing, the tourists and the "ethnic" teenagers noted elsewhere in this study took their place, and the Village became more and more folked up. The beat subculture in its original form still survives in parts of the lower East Side and elsewhere—although, for reasons too complex to relate here, on a greatly diminished scale.]

But an important secondary reason for the coffee shops is that in the last three years the attitudes of beats in their thirties have spread rapidly downward all the way to very young teenagers (13–15 years old), who need these shops because they are too young to fake their age in bars. About a fourth of those under 16 are fully beat and have totally abandoned, among other things, such square institutions for teenagers as parental home and school. The remainder are quasi-beat, not so much because they have doubts about beat life as because they are not yet able completely to escape parental control.

Some newer coffee shops are on the lower East Side (out of the Village proper) and a couple of that neighborhood's restaurants have also become fairly beat. In part this is the result of low-income Villagers moving eastward in the face of rising Village rents. But these shops cater also to beats from various parts of the city who want to avoid Village tourists. These beats, together with many others who go to Village coffee shops entirely or almost entirely during non-tourist hours, and still others—including most older beats—who rarely go to coffee shops at all (a great portion of beat social life takes place at private parties), comprise the large majority of beats.

[5] [An excellent description and discussion of the beat exodus from San Francisco is Ralph Gleason's "Begone, Dull Beats," *New Statesman,* June 2, 1961, p. 868.]

IV

Many beats are teenage runaways, but hardly any are being sought by the police; apparently most come from families that would just as soon be rid of them. But Village beats, teen-agers and otherwise, are not predominantly of lower-class parentage. Roughly 35 per cent are from the lower class and sixty per cent or a little more from the middle class. There is also a sprinkling (about 5 per cent) of upper-class renegades; as a group they seem the most psychologically disturbed of all beats and as often as not are remittance men, i.e., are sent money by their parents to stay away from home.[6]

The composition of the Village beat population today, com-pared with that of three years ago, shows several other changes in addition to the greatly increased number of young teenagers. A dozen or so Italian neighborhood kids are breaking away from Italian community values (always opposed to Vil-lage bohemians) and are attracted to the beats. And some Puerto Ricans are beginning to enter the beat scene; previously the only "American" group one found them in was the homosexuals.

Although a number of beat writers are of Jewish origin, the proportion of Jews among the white male beats has severely declined in the past three years, and in the Village beat scene they now seem to be considerably under-represented. Jewish women, on the other hand, are if anything over-represented. Otherwise there seems nothing unusual about the religious origins of the beats.

A few of the newer beat women are worn-out ex-prosti-tutes from the Times Square area, in their early twenties, who realized they had nothing to show for several years of hustling —no love, no money, no friendships. They want to escape the

---

[6] The above percentages are tentative estimates, based on quite sketchy material concerning family origins. I used the following rough-and-ready class definitions: lower-class origin if parents' annual com-bined income was under $4500; middle class, $4500–$9000; upper class, $9000 or more.

hustling scene but of course have difficulty adjusting to a square scene, and hence are attracted to the beats, toward whom they are motherly. Conversely, a few beat men hustle themselves a couple of nights a week in uptown homosexual bars, making enough money to stay straight in the Village the rest of the week. In one way this last is typical of the odd job the beat takes when, despite all his efforts to avoid it, he must work: he doesn't want to be *seen* working by other beats, and prefers a job away from the beat scene (except that it is considered all right to work in a beat coffee shop).

But the biggest change in the composition of the Village beat scene, and in Village life generally, is the far greater absolute number and far greater percentage of Negroes.

Until about three years ago there were few Negroes in the Village and they were forced to have their own bar, Johnny Romero's. Romero's paid off the syndicate after several broken windows reminded the owner of this civic duty, and of course paid the police, but was eventually closed because it got too hot to handle (one of the bar's prostitutes was discovered to be a juvenile runaway from a prominent family).

Today, hundreds of Negroes can be found in any number of Village coffee shops and bars, some of which, e.g., Polelle's,[7] function mainly as places for Negroes who want white girls to pick up same. The Negroes around Polelle's haven't much in common except such desires, and range from very beat to Ivy League types. The only thoroughly beat Negro scene is the Maracanda, where most of the clientele are junkies and Charlie Parker is the squarest thing on the jukebox.

V

On the increase in the Village and its east-side adjunct are beats with literally no place to live, without even a slum

[7] In this essay Village commercial establishments frequented by beats appear pseudonymously, except for one bar now defunct.

sleeping-room. I'd guess that at any given time these homeless beats number not less than 150.

To sleep, some drop in on friends who live in cheap lofts; often there will be ten or twelve people sleeping on a loft floor. Or they sleep in tenement hallways—the top landing, just inside the door to the roof, being the usual choice for beats (unlike homeless alcoholics, who usually must choose the less secure ground level because they can't make it up the stairs). In warm weather there are rooftops; or parks, where one has a 50–50 chance of not being awakened by the police. And some beats sit out the wee damp hours in Smith's, one of the restaurants in the area.

For several years Smith's has been a favorite place for junkies and marihuana smokers to meet their connections. But it has been very hot ever since the police stationed an informer there and one night arrested eleven people, and since then it has had a fink or more or less permanent detail. The first fink uncovered by the beats and junkies was replaced; but at this writing the police haven't bothered to replace his replacement, and the current fink, who is known to all the regular customers and knows that he is known, often gets baited with stage whispers of "Can anybody turn me on?" etc.

VI

Naturally, the Italian residents of the Village are going down fighting.[8] The older ones, upset by the noise and the Negroes, this summer petitioned their political chiefs to do something—whereupon two of the most prominent coffee shops were closed by the Fire Department for violations, one of them later being permitted to reopen at half its former capacity. (The shops selected were of course non-Italian, though hardly

[8] "Italian" refers mainly to Sicilians, the dominant Village ethnic group, whose criminal minority controls Village nightlife and is prominant in the national crime syndicate, not to Neapolitans living south of the Village.

any commercial establishment within blocks of the area doesn't
have fire violations.) However, contrary to the opinion of some
beats, it is doubtful that the syndicate had anything to do with
the closings, for long ago the syndicate put aside its anti-Negro
feelings in favor of its commercial interests and declared itself
in for a piece of the beat pie. Except for a few upper-class
places north of Washington Square, every Village coffee shop
or bar or restaurant, beat or non-beat, pays "grease" to the
syndicate as well as to the cops.[9]

Many younger Italians of course make violent efforts to roll
back the beat invasion, especially during summer with everyone in the streets. Most of the violence is directed against
Negroes and much of it is focused in and near the main beat
crossroads, Washington Square Park. The kids under twelve
usually restrict themselves to throwing water bombs and feces
down on the beats from Macdougal Street rooftops; but more
than occasionally beats are also slugged by junior hoodlums
from the local Catholic Youth Organization—described by one
beat as America's only juvenile gang with a lawyer on retainer.
The daily newspapers, except for the New York *Post,* ignore
such things as much as they can, and even the *Post* dare not

[9] Syndicate enforcement methods are the well-publicized strongarm
ones. Less known are the police methods for handling those who contribute too little or the rare idealist who contributes nothing at all. These
methods are nonviolent, flexible, and various. Among them are "dis-
orderly premises" (almost anything will make it stick), "finding" heroin
in the place—one astonished response: "Man, don't crucify me, you
know I only smoke pot"—and having a New York newspaper columnist
blast the place until the owner comes across or the police are "forced"
by the publicity to raid him.

Given the system's values, the method chosen usually represents
a quite rational police estimate as to how severely the holdout needs
to be punished—whether it is best to just scare him, or have him fined,
or cause him expensive repairs, or close him for a bit, or have the
State Liquor Authority lift his liquor license, or send him to jail. Occasionally irrational factors are involved, such as one cop's invariable
method of operation or another's sadism. Much less frequently, there is
also an "outside" factor, e.g., public outcry leading to pressure from
high brass, or an owner's strong political connections, or the owner of,
say, an established homosexual bar being outbid by someone else who
wants to obtain the local homosexual business.

offend part of the readership by mentioning the C. Y. O.; nor, for that matter, can the *Village Voice*.

I summarize one of many incidents:

A beat couple are set upon and stomped by the C. Y. O. gang. The police arrest the beats along with some of their attackers. The beats of course can't make bail. As a result of the beating the girl has a miscarriage while in the Women's House of Detention. The cops, discovering that the girl is underage, point out to the couple that if anyone talks about the miscarriage they will have to charge her as a sexual delinquent and him as contributing to her delinquency. At the hearing every-one plays it cool and all are released. But the police have the judge lecture the male beat that he is barred from the Village and will be rapped the next time he's found there, so now he stays east of Third Avenue. This has raised his status in the eyes of some: "A way out bit, man. I mean, lots of studs've been eighty-sixed from bars but he's the first one eighty-sixed from the whole fucking Village."

Some beats have correctly observed that opposition to them is in part displaced hostility toward another "invading" group that the Italians can't fight effectively because it is too rich: the uptown squares who are tearing down low-rent Village housing, moving into fancy buildings that Italians can't afford, and in the process of wresting local political control from the DeSapio machine.

VII

Beats avoid work. Contrary to what I expected among the non-junkies, this avoidance is typically not a rationalization for any kind of work incapacity (such as one finds in, say, the neurotic sleeper who can't get up in the morning), but is almost always a matter of conviction pure and simple. This conviction is so strong that many beats are willing to starve for it. Consequently, even among the non-junkies there is widespread malnutrition, and some instances of beat "passivity" seem to owe as much to lack of food energy as anything else.

Since an important factor in some kinds of retreatism is an inability to meet job norms (whether legitimate or criminal), it should be emphasized that beats typically can meet such norms but voluntarily choose not to do so. True, most beats are decidedly neurotic; and because they generally refuse their chances for either job training or college education, they can get only low-skilled jobs. But their intelligence and native talents are likely to be superior when not average, and their neuroses usually do not as such incapacitate them for holding jobs. Furthermore, their ideological refusal to work is not essentially a product of neurosis, even for the most neurotic of them, but is largely cultural in origin. (In this respect beats remind one of professional criminals, who may or may not be neurotic but whose neuroses usually have little to do with the genesis of their criminality.)

[Sociologists' response to the foregoing paragraph—or rather their total lack of response to it—greatly disappointed me. At the time of original publication I assumed sociologists would fasten on that paragraph above all others, since it was the first writing to question the general applicability of the double-failure theory of retreatism—and to do so on the basis of genuine field study of a genuinely "retreatist" delinquent subculture. But nobody picked up on it.]

Unlike most of their age-mates, beats are keen critics of the society in which they have grown up. Their anti-work ideology is not nearly so much a sign of inability to accept the reality principle as a sign of disaffiliation from particular, mutable realities. Sensible of America's inequitable distribution of income *and* its increasing depersonalization of work and leisure *and* its racial injustices *and* its Permanent War Economy, the beats have responded with the Permanent Strike. This response happens to be tragically mistaken, destructive of the self as well as incapable of provoking social change; but it is a virtuous error, arising out of dismay at things that are rotten in the social fabric.

A few beats live off parents or girlfriends and are "social parasites" as pure as anyone living off dividend checks. Most beats scuffle; they take jobs temporarily when all else fails,[10] but exist most of the time by combining panhandling, quick moves from one pad to another to beat the rent, a complex round of borrowings and repayments, short cons such as selling marihuana that is heavily cut, and so on. This freedom from routine work is bought at an enormous price: not only does scuffling often consume more time and brainpower than a square job,[11] but its effect on leisure is more stultifying than any job dissatisfaction would be.

Beats believe that voluntary poverty is an intellectual gain; they gain by giving up the evil effects of meaningless work, gadgetry and the mass media. But the net effect on their leisure is that even the most ardent intellectuals among them often can't spare the carfare to get to the better free libraries and concerts and art exhibits, seldom can attend cultural events for which admission is charged, and never can build up reasonable book and record libraries of their own. Their meager amount of intellectual consumption is not only questionable as such, but of course also stunts their growth as intellectual producers. "Holy poverty" enforces comparative poverty of the mind.

A number of times I used the above argument with beats, and got variants of one response: better to have a poorer intellectual life than get caught up in the rat race. And with the rare beat who conceded that the rat race occasionally could, with much prodding, be made to yield up work meaning-

[10] Beats quit jobs as soon as possible, seldom working a total of four months per year. But most beats of several years' standing have at one time or another—usually just once—tried the expedient of working barely long enough in a given year to be eligible for unemployment compensation. Informants recently on the west coast say that because Hawaii is now a state and one can collect unemployment benefits there, it is, among those beats who can scrape up boat fare, becoming increasingly popular as against Mexico.

[11] This and other intelligent objections to the beat lifestyle can be found in the anonymous "open letter to the beats from a spy deep in enemy territory," *Beatitude* No. 15, June 1960 (San Francisco), pp. 17–20.

ful in itself, the argument quickly became the old interminable one about the virtues of remaining simon pure vs. "boring from within," with the beat being confirmed in his purity as approaching daylight reminded me to stagger off for a couple of hours' sleep before rejoining the rat race.

VIII

I looked hard for changes in the beat attitude toward politics, but found instead confirmation of my old impression that it is wrong to describe the beats as apolitical *lumpen* who are potential fascists (Malaquais) or potential socialists (Mailer).

Far from being *lumpen,* beats are more keenly aware of the range of political alternatives than is the average voter. They are not apolitical but consciously and deliberately *anti*political, which is something else entirely, and, as a common attitude, something new in American history. Beats suffer not from political apathy but from political antipathy. They totally "resign" from society in so far as this is possible, not least of all from its politics, and reject extreme political sects with no less vigor than they reject major parties.

It might seem reasonable to call the beat an anarchist, for he objects to representative government on the same ground that Proudhon did, i.e., that no man can truly "represent" another man's thoughts and feelings—but more important is the fact that the beat doesn't want to promote anarchism or any other ism.[12]

All this has some virtues of its defects. If it means that the beat rejects any rational political planning, it means equally that he is not going to be a sucker for any charismatic leader whether of the right or left. [Here I was wrong. A little while

[12] In this respect as in some others, it is misleading to rely on the beat literary record, where one can, occasionally, find a quasi-political stance. Those who see the beats exclusively through their literature should remember that over 90 per cent of the beats neither write for publication nor wish to do so.

after this study was made, some beats became enamored of
Fidel Castro, and not only because of his tweaking the lion's
tail: they also concluded that he must be hip and use marihuana because he sported a ragged beard and refused to wear
a suit.[13] These beats became quickly disenchanted with Castro
as soon as his particular brand of authoritarianism set in.] Of
course the beat is pleased to see beat attitudes spread, but he
isn't interested in joining any organized social movement
toward that end. Each of the three words "organized social
movement" sounds obscene to the beat's ears.[14] And though
naturally amused to see some of his fellows such as Allen
Ginsberg achieve notoriety and shake up the squares, he doesn't
regard Ginsberg or anyone else as his "spokesman" (much
less "leader") in the sense that squares conceive of spokesman-
ship. The beat's only spokesman is himself.

American intellectuals, and those of European origin especially, misunderstand this because they are prone to see every
irrational excrescence in American political life as a sign of
fascism round the corner (recall the panicky overinterpreta-
tions of MacArthur's "triumphal" return from Korea, etc.).
To those who insist on finding a German ancestor for the
beats, I would suggest that the proper ancestor is not the

[13] [This beat error was overmatched at the time by *Playboy* dim-
wits, who concluded that John Kennedy must be hip and use marihuana
because of his Hollywood friends and some other matters.]

[14] In view of my earlier finding (*Dissent,* Winter, 1958) that the
beats are not totally atomized individuals but instead form a subculture,
they must of course have some social organization. But it is of the
most tenuous sort. The beat group approximates the *primitive band* as
described by Ralph Linton: a group of fairly constant membership
larger than the family, compact, nomadic but exploiting a fairly well-
defined territory, socially self-sufficient and facing inward, without *rites
de passage,* without formal governmental machinery, etc.

The last two features (perhaps the last three) distinguish the beat
group sharply from the gang. Although Lewis Yablonsky in "The
Violent Gang" (*Commentary,* August, 1960) claims that today's gang
"lacks all features of an organized group," he goes on to contradict
himself by describing types of gang officers and their duties, etc. The
very concept of office is nonexistent in any beat group. [This difficulty
with Yablonsky's view of the gang has since been noted independently
by Ralph England, in *American Journal of Sociology,* Vol. LXX, No. 5
(March, 1965), p. 630.]

storm trooper but rather the philosopher-poet Friedrich Nietzsche, who correctly described himself as "an ardent anti-
antisemite," as "opposed to everything that calls itself *Reichs-
deutsch,*" and as "the last anti-political German."

If the three hundred and more beats I talked with are in
any way representative, then many of their journalistic detrac-
tors—sometimes misled by ambiguities in Norman Mailer's
"The White Negro"—have made utterly false equations between the teenage hoodlum and beat worlds. These armchair
social analysts need to catch up with current sociological theory
and learn the differences between "conflict" and "retreatist"
delinquent subcultures. Even more, they need to stop bombinat-
ing *in vacuo* and actually meet the people they write about—
if only to learn that for every beat who is unusually given to
violence there are at least two dozen beats who are sincere
pacifists.

IX

In the Village beat world, as in all bohemias by definition,
the socially disapproved forms of sexual behavior are tolerated
if not encouraged. And as one would expect in the current
bohemia, interracial intercourse is particularly frequent.

What one would not necessarily expect is the peculiar
pattern that homosexual behavior takes among the beats. Proportionately, the amount of such behavior seems as high as in
the non-beat world even though the beat whose outlets are
entirely or almost entirely homosexual is proportionately very
much rarer than his non-beat counterpart. In other words
an extraordinary number of male beats, whites as well as
Negroes, are fully bisexual or in some cases polymorphous
perverse.[15] They accept homosexual experiences almost as

[15] In terms of the Kinsey heterosexual-homosexual rating scale from
zero to six, beats show an unusual clustering at points two, three and
four. Cf. Alfred Kinsey, Wardell Pomeroy and Clyde Martin, *Sexual
Behavior in the Human Male* (Philadelphia: W. B. Saunders, 1948),
pp. 638–41.

casually as heterosexual ones. Even beats with numerous and continuing post-adolescent homosexual experiences typically do not feel the need to define themselves as homosexuals and create some sort of beat wing of the homosexual world. Nor do they give up heterosexual involvements. Beats not only tolerate deviant sex roles but, to a much greater extent than previous bohemians, display a very high tolerance of sex-role ambiguity.

Most likely this subcultural trait was originally transmitted to the white beats by Negro beats, for not only do Negroes set much of the tone of beat life, but Negro culture has always had a higher tolerance of sexual ambiguity than white culture, and also the non-beat white groups showing high tolerance (e.g., seamen, ex-convicts) have had a special conditioning factor—prolonged absence from women—that is lacking in the beat world.

The unusual breadth of beat sex life is accompanied by very little depth. All types of beats at all age levels fail to establish deep and lasting sexual relationships. Lack of virility, however defined, is a frequent problem among the white males (and a characteristic of all long-time junkies); this substantial minority is essential passive. The majority of beats, conversely, engage in an endless series of short-term affairs that bespeak much more of acting out than of action. Their bed-hopping "genitality" comes about precisely because they too are sexually impoverished—"orgastically impotent" in Reich's terms—and have yet to discover that in sex life there is no automatic passage from quantity to quality. Consequently, even among the oldest beats it is uncommon to find a couple who have been living together more than two or three years; and as often as not, such couples have managed to stick together only by replacing sex with the symbiotic cement of mutual drug addiction.[16]

[16] This is not to imply that junkie couples achieve long-run stability (the reverse doubtless is true), but rather that in its *initial* phases mutual addiction "helps keep the family together."

X

For obvious reasons beat drug-taking is a furtive affair, and hence few outsiders realize that it is a totally pervasive part of beat life, both as an activity and as a topic of conversation. The illegal use of drugs is one of the handful of things that characterize all male beats with very rare exceptions, and a good majority of the females. But contrary to some popular views, (a) the majority use non-addicting drugs exclusively and (b) the majority of such users do not eventually go on to use addicting drugs and become junkies.

I talked with about 285 male beats and directly or indirectly queried about 205 concerning their possible illegal use of drugs, of whom only 14 denied any such use whatever; of about 25 female beats queried, out of about 40 I talked with, 9 denied illegal use of any drug.[17] Some beats who denied such use were doubtless lying. Although for most beats I did not obtain data on frequency of use, it seems certain that the majority use drugs at least once every couple of days, whether the drugs are addicting or non-addicting or a combination. Many younger beats have been thoroughly socialized to drug-taking without ever having been socialized to drinking, and are teetotalers when it comes to alcohol.

Beats do not constitute the majority of those who use drugs illegally, but their lives often intersect with that majority at the points of supply. Consequently much of the information below, though gathered from Village beats, deals with general New York drug distribution.

A. Addicting Drugs. Heroin is the drug of choice among beat junkies, though a few are hooked on barbiturates. The other addicting opiates and synthetics—morphine, codeine, demerol,

---

[17] The figures are exact for those denying illegal use of drugs; the other figures are estimates, as I didn't start keeping strict count of these until part way through my investigation. My talks with beats were not formal interviews and varied considerably in length. With some beats in the sample I spent less than five minutes; with others, more than thirty hours.

dolophine, pantopon, etc.—are all used freely by junkies when available, but in the Village they are available less often than heroin or barbiturates, and no beat junkie seems primarily addicted to one of these drugs as such; rather, these drugs are used in addition to heroin or as substitutes for it.

Opium itself is often available. However, it is expensive ($15–20 for a *toy,* a ball about the size of a large pea) and beats regard it as something to try once for kicks but otherwise not worth the price—partly because it is less powerful than its main derivatives and partly because there is rarely an opium layout and experienced preparer available. A few beats claim there is still one old-style "opium den" in Chinatown, to which no whites or Negroes and very few Chinese are admitted. Although disappointed at being barred, they admire the Chinese for playing it so cool.

Apart from questions of secrecy, it is hard to estimate the percentage of junkies among the beats because there are marginal cases (those who use addicting drugs occasionally but have not become addicts) and because some addicts cannot yet admit to themselves, much less to an outsider, that they have been hooked. I counted as junkies not only those who indicated they were, but all admitted users of addicting drugs who indicated they had ever experienced withdrawal discomfort, whether or not they indicated that drugs had been taken to relieve such discomfort, and regardless of frequency of use.[18] By this criterion, among Village beats under 20, about one out of fifteen is a junkie; between 20 and 25, about one out of eleven; over 25, about one out of nine.

Off and on during the past year—though not at present —there have been in the Village severe shortages of heroin. Users unanimously state that this has not been due to an increase in Village arrests but entirely to another factor: some time ago the syndicate decided to pull out of the drug business

[18] A partial justification for this procedure is the statement of Lindesmith, *op. cit.,* p. 75: "The writer has never heard of a user who, having experienced the full intensity of the withdrawal symptoms in full knowledge of their relation to the absence of opiates, did not become an addict."

temporarily—this is partly what the Apalachin meeting was to be about—because of successful government prosecution of some very big shots (notably Stromberg) and harassment of others (notably Genovese).

Negroes and Puerto Ricans controlled some distribution in their neighborhoods but were not equipped to fill entirely the hole that the syndicate pullout left in their own supplies, much less take over distribution elsewhere. Apparently Negro and Puerto Rican areas at first felt the pinch as much as the Village, not merely because of the syndicate pullout but because many more white junkies began trying to score from them. Indeed, some white Village pushers and users of heroin moved to the racially mixed areas of the upper West Side and lower East Side.

When the syndicate pulled out, for some junkies there was at first total panic; their connections simply had no junk. Now all junkies can obtain heroin regularly again—a few believe that syndicate members previously unassociated with the drug traffic are entering it—but complain that the price has risen steeply in the form of greater dilution. (In the absence of actual analysis of drug samples, such statements should be treated with caution. Complaints about increasing dilution are always common among junkies, the main reason being the junkies' increasing tolerance of drugs.) Three junkies say that there have been a sharply increased number of sick junkies unable to support their habits at former levels, trying to taper off on such things as Cocinil, and hitting drugstores so often that some stores have been totally "burned down," i.e., refuse to supply even non-prescription items to known junkies.

[Shortly after this study was made, Vito Genovese was convicted on federal narcotics charges. Some time later, the most prominent figure in Greenwich Village organized crime, Anthony Strollo ("Tony Bender"), permanently disappeared, and crime reporters said this was retribution for his having refused the demand of higher-ups that he be cooler about heroin distribution and take the financial losses involved.]

B. Non-addicting Drugs. Beats frequently use non-addicting and non-hallucinatory stimulants, such as dexedrine; but their use of non-addicting drugs focuses invariably and overwhelmingly on the hallucinogens. Among these, marihuana is the drug of choice. Marihuana smokers also use peyote, hashish, and synthetic mescalin in that order of frequency. Recently a few marihuana smokers have experimented with using peyote exclusively for extended periods. Cocaine is seldom used because it is expensive and the "high" it produces does not last long; beats say it is a rich man's drug, used mostly in wealthy show business and criminal circles.

Beats who use no illegal drugs are few. To estimate the proportion using marihuana, it would not be far wrong to simply reverse the above estimates concerning beat junkies. Thus, among beats under 20, marihuana smokers would outnumber junkies nearly fourteen to one; between 20 and 25, nearly ten to one; over 25, nearly eight to one.[19] About a

[19] These estimates differ astoundingly from those usually found in the literature on narcotics, where it is typically estimated that about 91½ per cent of all New York drug users known to authorities use addicting drugs and about 8½ per cent use non-addicting drugs such as marihuana. Cf. *Second Interim Report of the State of New York Committee on Narcotic Study,* Legislative Document (1958), No. 16, p. 12.

There are several possible reasons for the discrepancy, all of which might be operative here: (a) Though I tried to secure a representative sample of beats, junkies may have been slightly under-represented. (b) Some beats who are junkies doubtless kept this fact hidden from me. (c) Beats are somewhat unrepresentative of New York drug users generally, because nearly all the junkies attracted to New York from the rest of the country (New York is now estimated to have between one-third and one-half of America's junkies) probably go to non-beat circles. (d) The number of New York marihuana smokers may indeed be several times the number of junkies, but the latter pose such a severe problem that narcotics police must give them near-total attention, and hence marihuana smokers rarely come to the attention of the authorities. (This would follow from the beat testimony cited below, which there seems no reason to doubt, concerning the pattern of narcotics arrest.) (e) Additional support for the view that marihuana smokers may greatly outnumber junkies is that the latter often must turn to crime to support their habits and/or turn themselves in for treatment—both of which bring them to the attention of the authorities—whereas marihuana smokers do neither.

The one other comparative survey of drug use I know of that does not depend on arrest rates also finds that marihuana smokers outnumber heroin users, though the differences are not nearly as startling. Cf. Charles Winick, "The Use of Drugs by Jazz Musicians," *Social Problems,* Vol. VII, No. 3 (Winter, 1959–60), especially p. 242.

dozen men and two women stated that most beat women smoke marihuana but few are real "potheads" (devotees of marihuana), and that most smoke it mainly because their men do.

Although beat heroin users and beat marihuana smokers are part of one subculture, they tend to split into two separate groups when it comes to the specific activity of taking drugs, each developing its own customs.

As Howard Becker has shown, marihuana smoking is a group activity in which the psychic response to the drug in large part has to be taught to the newcomer.[20] (It appears that marihuana is a drug in which tolerance not only does not go up, but as a result of learning actually goes down.) Beat marihuana smokers not only confirm this, but indicate that even after the user has internalized the group's norms and thus can get high alone, his drug-taking continues to have a much more social quality than that of the heroin user. One made a remark that would be almost inconceivable from a heroin user: "Sometimes it's okay to get high by yourself, but then I always like to go out and bounce it off other studs." Beat statements about group marihuana-using sessions and group heroin-using sessions consistently indicate a far greater degree of mutuality in the former, particularly with regard to both verbal and nonverbal sharing of drug-induced psychic states.[21] It is possible that this mutuality has a strong latent homosexual component and that this is what bars most female beats from full participation; the four beats I asked about this thought there was something to it.

Narcotics police in the Village, say the beats, used to spend all their time chasing junk (addicting drugs). Marihuana users were safe if they stayed on their own scenes, and were arrested only if they were discovered accidentally—typically if they were on a junk scene when the police came looking for junk.

---

[20] Howard S. Becker, "Becoming a Marihuana User," *American Journal of Sociology,* Vol. LIX (November, 1953), pp. 235–42.

[21] This psychic sharing among marihuana smokers reaches its peak in the "contact high." Cf. Winick, *op. cit.,* p. 244.

This is still generally true, but beats note that in the past year there have been two major Village raids on strictly marihuana-smoking groups. And the police forced the one coffee shop that earlier this summer was selling peyote openly (not against New York State law) to discontinue sales, by invoking a city health ordinance concerning potentially poisonous foods.

During the past four months (May through August) there have been recurrent shortages in the Village marihuana supply. These shortages have been more frequent and of longer duration than heroin shortages, a situation the beats say is truly extraordinary: "Man, there's never been anything like it. All the smack you want and a complete pot panic." [22] To obtain marihuana at all, beats have sometimes been forced to buy it in a form (already rolled into "joints," rather than loose) and at a price (75 cents or $1 per joint) that they say are usually reserved for the rich college crowd. There are many stories about marihuana being cut with bay leaves, oregano, etc., and about an increase in the number of "burns" (in which someone who claims he can obtain drugs takes money in advance and never returns).[23]

Beats feel that the marihuana shortages, unlike those of heroin, have little to do with the syndicate lying low, for the distribution of marihuana has always been almost entirely independent of syndicate control. The consensus is that marihuana supplies have not decreased, and may even have increased, but in recent months have had to be spread over a suddenly expanding market.

The horde of new teenage beats, many just arrived in the

[22] "Smack" is one of several terms for heroin. Marihuana is usually "pot," though "boo" and other terms are sometimes heard. "Panic," usually in the form of "there's a panic on," means that there is a drug shortage. The argot is of course subject to rapid change. For humorous effect, beats will sometimes use a term that is no longer current except among square writers: "Got a reefer, man?"

[23] Some older drug users say the greater number of burns is due to the increased mobility of today's beats. Beats are in fact more mobile than old-style hoboes. Not only do they shuttle between New York and California, but they have their own "international set" whose principal stopping places are in Mexico, the Balearic Islands, Tangier, and Paris.

Village this summer, nearly all use marihuana.[24] Moreover, while the Village beat market has been expanding, some of its normal supplies have been deflected to new markets elsewhere. Beats say that the use of marihuana in white non-beat circles was until recently pretty much restricted to jazz musicians and theater people, but that in the past year it has been spreading rapidly in the worlds of advertising, radio-TV, college students, etc.—the *Playboy* readership, essentially—and that some suppliers formerly in the Village have shifted to the favorite hangouts of these groups because they pay more. It is said that some ex-Village pushers of marihuana and hashish now work the fancy uptown East-Side bars, and that earlier this summer two Village pushers took off for Provincetown when they discovered that what would be a $5 bag of marihuana in the Village was selling for $15 to the Provincetown sportscar set.

[The beats' most enduring imprint on American culture appears, in retrospect, to have been precisely this diffusion of marihuana use to many circles of middle- and upper-class whites outside the jazz world. Such contemporary white use, although now self-sustaining and still growing, stemmed largely from public attention given to beat practices and beat literary proselytizing on the matter. The accompanying chart—which represents, as near as I can determine at this time, the history of marihuana use in America—illustrates the role of the beats as the key transmission belt for the current white use of marihuana.

The beats managed to do what some scientific investigators of marihuana had tried but failed to do: they convinced many sectors of the American public that the Federal Narcotics

[24] In the opinion of some beats, which I share, the new teenage beats will end up producing proportionately fewer junkies than older groups have done. This is *not* because they are aware that "just fooling round" with heroin almost always leads to addiction, for there is hardly a heroin addict alive who didn't know that to begin with. It is rather that among beats today the use of heroin has lost much of its glamor, is less often considered a requisite of being hip, and frequently is even considered "uncool." A similar change seems to have taken place in the ideology of jazz musicians. Cf. Winick, *op. cit.*, *passim*.

THE SPREAD OF MARIHUANA USE IN AMERICA
Culture Contact, Differential Association, and Subcultural Diffusion

MEXICO

↓

SOUTHWESTERN U.S.

(intro. about 1910 by Mexican laborers; becomes established among Mexican-Americans; sporadic cowboy use, but doesn't become established there)

↓

NEW ORLEANS

(intro. to Negroes, via Mexican-Americans, by 1920)

↓

URBAN NEGRO LOWER CLASS, SOUTH & NORTH

(well established by late 1920's; rapid spread begins about 1931)

NEGRO JAZZ MUSICIANS* & NEGRO FANS (simultaneously with other Negroes, as above)

WHITE LOWER CLASS IN RACIALLY MIXED NEIGHBORHOODS (some by mid-1930's, but mostly since late 1940's)

WHITE JAZZ MUSICIANS & WHITE FANS (some by late 1920's; rapid spread among white musicians in mid-1930's, but not among fans until "hipsters" of early 1940's and "beat" fans from about 1948 onward)

NON-MUSICIAN WHITE ENTERTAINERS (some by early 1930's; mainly nightclub & stripper subcultures—incl. criminals & prostitutes assoc. with those industries—but also some movie, circus, & legit. theatre people)

"BEATS" GENERALLY

(by 1950; incl. the minority not especially devoted to jazz)

WHITE MIDDLE- & UPPER-CLASS PSEUDO-BOHEMIANS (late 1950's; *Playboy* types, e.g., sportscar set, "hippy" adv. copywriters)

WHITE "ETHNIC" & "FOLK" TEEN-AGERS, FOLKSY-ARTSY CIRCLES (late 1950's)**

WHITE COLLEGE STUDENTS (some by 1950; rapid spread since 1960)

WHITE MIDDLE- & UPPER-CLASS HIGH SCHOOL STUDENTS (mainly since 1961)

---

* The earliest of many jazz records whose titles refer to marihuana is Louis Armstrong's *Muggles* (OK 8703), recorded December 7, 1928. ("Muggles" is an obsolete argot term for marihuana.) The titles of four earlier jazz records refer to other drugs: Josie Miles's *Pipe Dream Blues* (1924), Bennie Moten's *Goofy Dust* (1924), Duke Ellington's *Hop Head* (1927), and Victoria Spivey's *Dope Head Blues* (1927). I take these from Charles Delaunay's *New Hot Discography* (New York: Criterion Music Corp., 1948), but have not been able to check through Brian Rust's later and fuller discography.

References to marihuana also occur in the lyrics, but not the titles, of other early jazz records, e.g., Bessie Smith's *Gimme a Pigfoot* (1933).

** Many post-1960 references to marihuana can be found in recordings by white "folk" and "rock" singers (Bob Dylan, the Rolling Stones, *et al.*).

Bureau's myths about marihuana—the notions that marihuana is a significant cause of crime, insanity, and heroin addiction—were indubitably myths.[25]

Some other hallucinogens not mentioned in my study were taken up by the beats in 1961 and have since then spread elsewhere. But recent publicity about increasing use of the most powerful such drug, LSD-25, has tended to obscure the fact that marihuana use has been, and still is, increasing much more. From estimates made for me by students on several college campuses, I would judge that among college students the number of regular marihuana users is at least twenty times the number of regular LSD users—and this despite the fact that over half the college marihuana users apparently have also tried LSD at least once.

With the rise of marihuana use among college students has come its acceptance, in a sense, by college administrators. Especially in the large schools, officials tend increasingly to "look the other way" and do nothing whatever about marihuana-using students unless pressured by police or parents or newspaper publicity.

Proselytizers for marihuana—beats and college users alike —interpret all this to mean that marihuana will be adopted by ever-widening segments of the population and one day replace liquor in the affections of most Americans. They are unhappy when I tell them that the only age group being affected in significant degree is the one most given to passing

---

[25] [Although the better-educated segment of the public is now aware of the myths for what they are—knows, for example, that the myriads of college students who currently smoke marihuana are not thereby "led to" heroin addiction—this has in no wise lessened the efforts of the Federal Narcotics Bureau to perpetuate the myths and otherwise to suppress the scientific evidence of marihuana's harmlessness. The Bureau's undiminished efforts have convinced a number of sociologists, including myself, to come round to the view long maintained in heroic isolation by Alfred Lindesmith of Indiana University, viz., that some Bureau officials are not dedicated truthseekers having honest differences of opinion with the academic investigators, but on the contrary dedicate themselves first and last to extending the power of the Federal Narcotics Bureau—to the extent of deliberate falsification of evidence.]

fads, that smoking marihuana may be to this college generation what swallowing goldfish was to another, and that college
students twenty years from now may have as little interest in
marihuana as they did twenty years ago.]

IX

Almost all Village beats technically are literate, and some
whites have even attended college, but at best a sixth are
habituated to reading (none seem addicted) and far fewer are
concerned with writing. (Most square articles on "the beats"
go astray because beat writers, being highly visible, get all the
attention and thus a small and atypical part is taken for the
whole.) Among the minority who could be called regular
readers, the "literary" materials read consist almost wholly of
writing by romantic hedonists, much of it third-rate or worse
and nearly all of it contemporary.

Interest in Zen passed its peak over a year ago and has
radically declined. In the Village at least, Zen now appears
to have been a beat fad whose only lasting significance in
American intellectual history is that it (along with jazz-cum-
poetry) marks the first time that a west coast bohemia exerted
a major influence on an eastern one. About the only carryover
from earlier mystical concerns is that some beats continue to
take an interest in divination; but formerly beats used the *I
Ching, or Book of Changes* for this purpose, whereas now
one finds the use of Tarot cards or some Harlem-derived
routine.

Insofar as most beats, whites and Negroes alike, can be
said to have a dominant intellectual interest, it is jazz music.
And the jazz world is the single non-beat segment of American
society that often attracts beats. (Their admiration for it is not
requited, to judge by musicians' complaints.) The nature and
depth of the beats' relation to jazz have remained unchanged
over the past three years, except that these years have produced some new heroes (e.g., Ray Charles) and a new villain

(for some beats, Ornette Coleman has replaced Dave Brubeck as the arch-fraud).

Although the white beat's attraction to the jazz world is often the very core of his "white Negro" role, there is little uniquely "beat" about all this. Such involvement is socially not very different from the relationship of adolescent whites to Negro jazz in several American non-beat and pre-beat bohemias. [Even the "white Negro" concept itself is old. A critic noted in 1930 that white jazzmen of the early 1920's, such as Bix Beiderbecke, "felt as a reality the spirit of negro blues. Indeed, such bands as the Wolverines were called 'white niggers.' " [26]] For example, nearly twenty years ago [i.e., 1942], when I was v.-p. of my high school jazz club, a 13-year-old zoot suiter, we often used to make the Harlem "balcony scenes" —boosting old Bessie Smiths and Hot Fives from the balcony of the Rainbow Music Shop before the wartime scrap drive wrecked the supply, going wild in the Apollo Theatre's sweet-smelling second balcony—odoriferous from pomade and pot, though we didn't know about the latter at the time—to a Basie-Millinder twin bill. And we traveled Swing Street when it still swung (where half the time we'd get kicked out despite our borrowed I.D.'s), to hear Billie Holiday at the Onyx Club or Tatum at the Three Deuces. Today, the big boosting scenes are Goody's and the Colony instead of the Rainbow; Swing Street has been replaced by scattered Village clubs; the white intellectual jazz mentors are Nat Hentoff and Martin Williams instead of Ralph Berton and Gene Williams; there are goatees instead of 12-inch peg pants, etc. But apart from the music itself, and the fact that now one merely listens to it at Birdland instead of stomping to it at the Savoy, not much has really changed.

[26] [Charles Edward Smith, "Jazz," *The Symposium*, Vol. 1, No. 4 (October, 1930), p. 509.]

XII

A few beats, invariably among the youngest, are not so much interested in jazz as in the folk music of the "ethnic" set. But all beats reject the folksy-artsy group as people because in fundamental attitude the latter, despite the number of Negroes among them, are un-or anti-beat.[27] The Village devotees of ethnic music are historically minded, scholarly, middle-class youths, mostly Jewish, who are trying to disown their parents' culture not by becoming beat but rather by proving that ancient proverb, "New York ain't America."

The intersection of beat and "ethnic" circles, and indeed of Village social circles generally, can be seen at its warm-weather wildest in the hundreds of people who on Sunday afternoons gather round the children's wading pool in Washington Square Park. The circles here are as much concentric as intersecting.

The inner circle consists of people who arrive by 1:00 P.M. and thus get seats on the rim of the pool and on the steps leading down into it; this circle is a mixture of early-rising square Villagers, many of whom have brought their children to wade, and beats who get there early because they've been up all night. (The beats used to get high and roll around in the pool with the kiddies, fully clothed, until the Park Department enforced the rule restricting the pool's use to those under 12 years of age.) Surrounding this is a second, standing circle of clusters of folk and hillbilly performers and their listeners: uptown tourists and new-style rich Villagers, "ethnic" teenagers, Italians, a few beats. Around this is a third circle, also quite mixed but consisting mostly of beats asking each other what's happening, tourists with cameras trying to elbow their way into the second circle for a good shot, and tight-trousered Village homosexuals walking their dogs and cruising each other.

[27] When the Fire Department raided beat coffee shops, the proprietor of The Folklore Center on Macdougal Street went so far as to issue a mimeographed broadside (dated June 12, 1960) praising this action and condemning the beats. Shortly thereafter he had his window broken.

XIII

In going through a good-sized collection of beat and semi-beat little magazines, published in various cities here and abroad, I have been unable to find 150 writers who by any definition could be called beat. Given the fact that beat writers are not notably reluctant to take the first things that pop into their heads and send them out to the world (if only via the mimeograph machine), and that on a most conservative estimate there cannot be less than 2000 beats in New York alone, it would be charitable indeed to say that a tenth of the beats are concerned to write. But today in the Village and elsewhere, significantly more beats are writing than was the case three years ago, and it seems that now at least as high a proportion of them are writing as was true of earlier bohemians.[28] In four or five cases their motives are not of the highest—come to no more than the knowledge that one can pick up some change by reciting shockers to tourists in coffee shops—but most are sincere about their writing, and in any event whatever literary talent there may be among the beats now stands a good chance of being discovered.

Most beat literature is poor when it is not godawful. And this is certainly true of its best-publicized examples, which have been surpassed even by the minor Victorians: James Thomson's poetic howl of urban despair, *The City of Dreadful Night,* is greater by far than anything Ginsberg offers,[29] and in on-the-road literature the genuine gusto of George Borrow, for all his prudishness, is preferable to the faked-up fervor of Kerouac. As for the beat talk of achieving a "break-

[28] Still far less than 10 per cent, however. In thinking of past bohemias we tend to recall only accomplishments and forget that for, say, every Village bohemian of the 1930's who actually sat down and wrote, there were several others just talking about it and a couple of dozen others doing not even that. Artists by definition know how to play, and hence attract many people who want to play all the time, which in turn makes it harder for artists to get their work done.

[29] *Howl* will remain important in our literary history as the most influential programmatic statement of a beat worldview. I deny merely that it is good poetry.

through" with respect to the old literary forms: this should be translated simply as "breakdown." The beats have not significantly extended the range of the old forms. And their contribution in the way of a new art form, if one can call it that, consists of bad poetry read to bad jazz, with not even an integration of the badnesses. That last point seems to have been realized by the beats themselves, for jazz-cum-poetry recitals occur infrequently these days.

Though a few beats regard Ezra Pound as one of their literary mentors, they see only the *épater l'académicien* side of him and don't dare face up to such typical Poundian dicta as: "Saxpence reward for any authenticated case of intellect having stopped a chap's writing poetry! You might as well claim the railway tracks stop the engine. No one ever claimed they would make it go." Beat writers start with a great deal against them. They are victims of a primitivist ideology that, in its oversimplified anti-academicism and anti-historicism, prevents many of them from reading much at all, prevents most of the others from reading anything written earlier than the day before yesterday, leads them into false and fatuous notions of "spontaneity," and keeps them from fully learning the technical skills involved in their art and fully exploiting whatever talents they may have. [In an interview granted in March, 1962, Pound himself put down the limited artistic purview of the mindless howlers who would misappropriate him. *"Interviewer:* 'You have given advice to young writers all your life. Do you have anything special to say to them now,' *Ezra Pound:* 'To improve their curiosity and not to fake. But that is not enough. The mere registering of bellyache and the mere dumping of the ashcan is not enough. In fact the University of Pennsylvania student *Punchbowl* used to have as its motto, 'Any damn fool can be spontaneous.' " [30]

The "spontaneity" nonsense may be discerned not only, or even primarily, in Kerouacian prose, but in the myriad beat poems written according to the new poetic that has received its most erudite expression in the "write like you breathe" and

[30] ["Ezra Pound: An Interview," *Paris Review,* Vol. 7, No. 28 (Summer-Fall, 1962), pp. 28–29.]

"composition by field" prosodic theory Charles Olson has elaborated.[31] Granted the obvious integrity of Olson himself, it remains true that "the importance of any theory," as P. W. Bridgman once remarked, "is what it actually does, not what it says it does or what its author thinks it does"—and that Olson's theory functions as a copout for poets with tin ears, with a defective sense of rhythm and structure. The theory put into practice gets rid of "artificiality" by getting rid of art.

And yet, the beat literary scene is not nearly as dismal as it was in 1957. For there *are* beats with genuine literary ability, and despite their cockeyed theories this ability is occasionally beginning to show itself. During the past three years the beats have produced some permanently valuable additions to American letters. (This is more than can be said for the entire output of some literary schools. Try reading, say, *Proletarian Literature in the United States*.) Among these writings are Gregory Corso's poem "Marriage," John Rechy's "The Fabulous Wedding of Miss Destiny" (one of the most dazzling American stories in years, and so genuinely distinctive that the editors of *Best American Short Stories, 1960* couldn't bear to put it in their also-ran list of "distinctive" stories, much less give it honorable mention or reprint it), and Jack Gelber's play *The Connection* (which acts much better than it reads).[32] And because the beats, unlike their French existentialist cousins and rather like the earlier Dadaists, see "the absurd" in its comic implications as fully as its tragic ones, a good deal of beat literature that fails as Art is quite enjoyable as Wisecrack.[33]

[31] Cf. Olson's essay reprinted in Donald Allen, ed., *The New American Poetry, 1945–1960* (New York: Grove Press, 1960), pp. 386–97.

[32] Corso's poem is most readily available in Allen, *op. cit.*, pp. 209–212. Rechy's story is in *Big Table*, Vol. 1, No. 3, 1959, pp. 11–39. *The Connection* is published by Grove Press. [Rechy's story has since been republished as part of his novel, *City of Night* (New York: Grove Press, 1963), pp. 102–129. I think it is the best part of the novel.]

[33] A recent example is "Wailing Wall for Richard Gumbiner—last seen," by Pierre Delattre and Alan Dienstag, in *Beatitude* No. 16 (July, 1960, no paging). This is the San Francisco magazine, not the rival *Beatitude* No. 16 published in New York by a defecting editor from San Francisco.

The beat writer with the most raw potential is Gregory Corso. True enough, he lacks a couple of technical craft skills (which can be taught) and sometimes falls into the worst clichés of thought as well as style. But unlike our slick young technicians Corso shows some real talents (which cannot be taught): he often does have something to say, usually makes you feel that *he* feels what he's saying, and displays in abundance a virtue that is the keystone of fine poetry—loving, imaginative play with language. Whether he will surpass the limits imposed by beat ideology or remain an extraordinarily gifted primitive is problematical.

XIV

Both white and Negro beats are notably given to calling a spade a spade. One would never catch them describing race relations as "intergroup" relations even if they knew the term, nor describing the lower class as the "working" class or old people as "senior citizens." But this forthrightness of speech and attitude, laudable as it may be, is not accompanied by much clarity of vision. Nowhere is there greater disparity between beat theory and practice than in the role that Negro beats, wittingly or unwittingly, are forced to play for white beats.

The several white beats I met who knew my earlier critique of them—unfortunately I met no Negro beats who knew it [34]— all disputed my claim that they accept the Negro only for his "Negro-ness" (as bringer of marihuana and jazz, etc.) and thus practice an inverted form of "keeping the nigger in his place." According to them, they really do accept the Negro in his totality. Maybe so; but I doubt it. White beats should be given credit for the best of conscious intentions, but it is dis-

[34] Some material that follows is touchy if not downright offensive to most Negroes, beat or non-beat. As I was able to explore all of it with only three Negro beats (two agreed completely, the other hedged on some parts), it should be regarded as subject to further proof or disproof.

heartening how often their actions confirm that old Negro proverb, "Whenever you see a white man with a colored man, the white man wants something from the colored man."

To see that Negroes living in the interracial beat world are still "invisible men" means to become sharply aware of something that white beats characteristically dodge: no modern urban Negro—raised as he is on white movies, white comic books, white television—can avoid internalizing white ideals, most especially can he not avoid internalizing white ideals of physical beauty, and on one level or another of his consciousness he puts himself down every time he looks in a mirror. (Hence the enormous Negro hair-straightening and skin-lightening industries, the profound discrimination among Negroes themselves on the basis of skin color, the high yellow beauty on the cover of *Ebony* who gives the lie to the magazine's title, etc.) Contrary to what many white beats believe, there is hardly a Negro alive who in his heart of hearts doesn't want to be white, and the various kinds of Negro chauvinist movements invariably represent a reaction formation against the forbidden desire to be white.

[As disproof of my claim that Negro chauvinist movements "invariably represent a reaction formation against the forbidden desire to be white," Nat Hentoff noted, in the April, 1962, issue of *Nugget,* that an increasing number of Negroes take conscious pride in being black. I replied (in *Nugget,* October, 1962, p. 8) as follows: "Mr. Hentoff's point does not at all contradict mine. I used 'reaction formation' in its technical psychoanalytic sense, which refers to an *unconscious* process. What I was trying to get at—the unconscious roots of conscious black chauvinism—is perhaps best indicated by the slip that one Negro chauvinist leader, Malcolm X, made on a TV interview program last November: 'I hate every drop of black blood —I mean *white* blood—that's in me.' "]

The modern American Negro's need to be white is one culture trait that the white male beat, like most of his square white brethren, cannot emotionally accept. This comes out most clearly, though not exclusively, in beat sex life; the Negro's desire for white girls is continually and subtly opposed by the white males, whatever their conscious beliefs may be, *not* merely in the terms with which one usually opposes a sexual rival but with such remarks as "X is too hung up on balling white chicks" or "Y's trouble is that he's too fay-oriented," and so on. Thus miscegenation in the beat world is essentially a conspiracy between white females and Negro males, that triumphs over strong white male opposition only because the latter can never become fully articulate since it contradicts the conscious ideology.

In addition to the remarks of white beats quoted above, there is evidence from the Negro side that all is not well.

Every Negro knows that the white man, though he dislikes all non-whites, has especially hostile feelings toward American Negroes; he knows experientially the truth in Max Weber's remark that the difference between the white man's attitude toward Indians and toward Negroes is that the Indians were never slaves. So the Negro who finds his status intolerable sometimes concludes that if he can't change his skin, at least he can try to escape his status as an *American* Negro—can try to enter some halfway house by pretending to be a Jamaican or Haitian or whatever. Recently the most influential halfway house among Negroes has been Islam.[35] These halfway houses are part of what Franklin Frazier calls the Negro "world of make-believe"—few Negroes or whites are really fooled by an American Negro's claim to be somebody else—but they do ease the pain somewhat. Now, it happens that several prominent jazz musicians have been converted to Islam. Statistically speaking, they represent a small portion of either American Negro Moslems or jazz musicians, and yet their presence has a real meaning, which is this: even if you're a very successful North-

[35] However, the emergence of West African nations is causing a shift among some Harlemites from a North African Moslem orientation to a West African non-Moslem one. See, for example, Priest Ofuntola Oserjeman, *Orisha: A First Glimpse of the African Religion of Brazil, Cuba, Haiti, Trinidad and now U.S.A.* (New York: Great Benin Books, African Library Series, n. d. [1960]), available from The Shango Temple, 71 East 125 Street.

ern Negro and move in circles that include many hip white admirers and make it with some cool white chicks, you're still expected to play it like a spade and it's still a drag.

The hip attitude toward Negroes is, to be sure, not only better than the usual square rejection of them but is superior to the phoney some-of-my-best-friends-are routines (which at best let in special performers of the arts, scholarship and politics under special conditions). And this ideology does mean that white beats meet with Negroes more often than white squares usually do. What is still questionable is the nature of these relationships.

Although the white beat grants the Negro a fuller role than other white "pro-Negro" groups do, he does it merely by compounding the limited roles those groups demand. For the white beat, the Negro fulfills the liberal's demand that he entertain plus the radical's demand that he symbolize the results of reactionary oppression plus the Harlem thrill-seeker's demand that he act out the primitive in all of us. One thing the Negro must *not* do is try to be white.

Instead of worrying about the Negro becoming "too fay-oriented" the white beats might consider accepting him in his inescapable aspect of Negro-wanting-to-be-white. They might even encourage it, for surely the only real solution to the psychological problems peculiar to the American Negro is the very solution that so worries our Southerners: miscegenation on a grand scale, the production of more and more Negroes who can pass, and ultimately the total "mongrelization" of the two races.

XV

I found it relatively easy to talk with beats, though the talk often had to be literally in their terms and representatives of the non-exhibitionist majority had to be diligently sought out: first, because they are typically more tolerant than political sectarians, more willing to accept an outsider who makes an honest attempt to understand them; second, because I agree with many of their criticisms of modern society; third, because from the onset of my own adolescence until a couple of years thereafter (at which time I enlisted in the death-struggles of Marxism), I and some of my friends went through a "white Negro" phase similar to that of many young beats today. However, if one makes it clear to the beats, as I did, that he is essentially a square, he will run into some who will give him a rough time, he will occasionally be put on (a combination of being conned and being baited). This was overcome in nearly all cases.

Generally, the only real hindrance proved to be that the beats, who by definition avoid work, are nightpeople. With respect to drugs there was the special problem that anyone investigating this area must of course convince the people involved that he is not a fink or a plain-clothesman, and I was not always able to do so. Thus the material on drugs, full as it may seem, is actually the thinnest part of my essay.

Nearly all beats I talked with at any length were told that I would write about them, and with four exceptions fairly easily accepted this. Nor was it necessary, except with a few paranoid-homicidal types, to keep from them my disagreements or the fact that what I wrote would in good part be critical.

5
On the Sociology of Pornography*

Samuel Johnson once informed James Boswell that he could recite a complete chapter of a book called *The Natural History of Iceland.* The chapter was entitled "Concerning Snakes," and consisted in its entirety of the following: "There are no snakes to be met with throughout the whole island." I can be similarly brief concerning studies on the sociology of pornography: there are no such studies to be met with throughout the whole of sociology.

What we do have, first of all, is an abundance of offhand "sociologizing" about pornography, on the part of contemporary journalists, cultural historians, psychiatrists, literary critics, lawyers, and judges—especially if they are of liberal inclination and don't like censorship. This material isn't worth much. In fact its chief interest for sociologists, as I shall elaborate below, is that the sociological interpretations most often found in it are demonstrably wrong.

Secondly, we have some published data on consumers of pornography and their social backgrounds. The best material of this sort, as on most matters sexual, comes (as you might expect) from the Institute for Sex Research.[1]

* Most of this chapter was presented at the annual meeting of the American Sociological Association, Miami Beach, August, 1966. I offered a sketchy first version of some of it at a public symposium, "Pornography and Literature," in which I participated with Alfred Chester, Benjamin De Mott, Ephraim London, and Hubert Selby, at the YMHA Poetry Center, New York City, March, 1966.
[1] Cf. Alfred Kinsey, Wardell Pomeroy, and Clyde Martin, *Sexual Behavior in the Human Male* (Philadelphia: W. B. Saunders, 1948), pp. 363, 510; and Kinsey, Pomeroy, Martin, and Paul Gebhard, *Sexual Behavior in the Human Female* (Philadelphia: W. B. Saunders, 1953), pp. 652–72. N. B. that most Kinsey findings on male use of pornography are presented in the volume on females, along with comparative data on females.

186

Thirdly, we have a particular sociological theory—I would call it a theory of the upper-middle range—that was not developed to explain the place of pornography in society but nevertheless serves, I think, to explain that place very well.

There are many special aspects of the sociology of pornography, and in what follows I shall not even mention most of them, much less pursue them. Instead, I shall try to spell out how that theory of the upper-middle range gives a sociological overview of pornography within which more specialized investigations might proceed.

I

In his study of prostitution Kingsley Davis demonstrated, with cogent reasoning and much evidence that I cannot rehearse here, the following main argument: (a) the goals of sexual behavior in man are not inherently social; but (b) societies need to hook sexuality onto social ends, particularly the ends of bearing and raising children, by restricting the morally legitimate expression of sex to the institution of the family; and (c) this conflict between sexual inclinations and social requirements is ameliorated by prostitution, which helps to maintain the family as an institution by acting as a safety-valve for the expression of antisocial coitus—i.e., impersonal, transitory, nonfamilial coitus—that cannot be fully suppressed.[2] Davis thus sees the family and prostitution as complementary institutions, each requisite to the other.

I suggest that Davis's theory applies, *mutatis mutandis,* to pornography. Prostitution and pornography occur in every society large enough to have a reasonably complex division of labor; and although pornography develops in only a rudimentary way in preliterate societies (by means of erotic folktales and simple pictorial or sculptural devices), whenever a society has a fair degree of literacy and mass-communication

[2] Cf. Kingsley Davis, "Prostitution," in Robert Merton and Robert Nisbet (Eds.), *Contemporary Social Problems* (New York: Harcourt, Brace & World, 1961), pp. 262–88.

technology then pornography becomes a major functional alternative to prostitution.

In saying that prostitution and pornography are, at least in modern societies, functional alternatives, I mean that they are different roads to the same desired social end. Both provide for the discharge of what society labels antisocial sex, i.e., impersonal, nonmarital sex: prostitution provides this via real intercourse with a real sex object, and pornography provides it via masturbatory, imagined intercourse with a fantasy object.

Although societies use both alternatives, the degree to which one is used in preference to the other seems to vary considerably from one society to the next, in ways and for reasons that remain to be investigated. There is also variation within a given society, of at least two kinds: First, there is variation in what is considered appropriate in different social situations; for example, a group of adolescent boys might collectively visit a prostitute but masturbate to pornography only singly and in private, with group contemplation of pornography serving merely to convey sex information or as the occasion for ribald humor. A second kind of variation has to do with what is considered appropriate in different subcultures. The main such variation in our own society, revealed by the Kinsey data, is that masturbating to pornographic books or pictures is largely a phenomenon of the better-educated classes; at the lower levels of our society, this is generally put down (as is long-term masturbation *per se*), and, conversely, prostitutes are visited much more often.

Prostitution, as Davis noted, presents a great paradox of social life: on the one hand it is so nearly a cultural universal that it seems to fill a need endemic to complex societies, but on the other hand the prostitute is, except in very special circumstances, generally and highly stigmatized. Davis's theory resolves the paradox, and does so in a way that applies equally to pornography: both prostitutes and pornographers are stigmatized because they provide for the socially illegitimate expression of sex, yet their very existence helps to make tolerable the institutionalizing of legitimate sex in the family.

An additional relation between the functioning and the stigmatizing of prostitutes and pornographers, a relation at once more general and more intimate than that given by Davis, may be inferred from the neo-Durkheimian theory of deviance recently proposed by Kai Erikson. He observes:

> The only material found in a system for marking [moral] boundaries is the behavior of its participants; and the kinds of behavior which best perform this function are often deviant. . . . In this sense, transactions between deviant persons and agencies of social control are boundary-maintaining mechanisms. . . . Each time the group censures some act of deviation it sharpens the authority of the violated norm. . . . [Instances of publicity about deviants, as in the old public parading of them or in the modern newspaper] constitute our main source of information about the normative contours of society [3]

In Erikson's view, then, one function of prostitutes and pornographers would lie precisely *in* the fact that they are stigmatized.

II

The use of pornography is by no means limited to its role as an adjunct to masturbation. For example, as already indicated, pornography may sometimes serve rather as a sex instruction manual. (Conversely, a sex instruction manual may serve as pornography.) And sometimes pornography, far from stimulating masturbation, may be used to stimulate real intercourse, as in, say, the case of whorehouse murals from Pompeii to the present. Granted all that, and other uses as well, people given to using pornography do so for the most part as a means of facilitating masturbation. This is the primary use of pornography. It is summed up in the classic description of pornographic books as "the books that one reads with one hand."

The consumption of pornography is a sort of halfway house

[3] Kai Erikson, "Notes on the Sociology of Deviance," *Social Problems,* Vol. 9 (Spring, 1962), pp. 307–14.

between sexual intercourse and erotic response to purely private mental fantasies. Masturbation to pornography is more "social" than masturbation simply to inner pictures, i.e., pornography offers the masturbator erotic imagery that is external to himself, a quasi-real "other" to whom he can more "realistically" respond. That is why even lower-class males frequently use pornography for masturbatory release—and here the Kinsey findings need qualification—when they are deprived of their usual sexual outlets: people in jails are overwhelmingly from the lower class, and the masturbatory use of pornography is widespread in jails and a continual headache for any prison administrator who wants to make it one.[4] Sociologists, however, in their fascination with the way prisoners turn toward homosexuality, seem to have neglected the prisoners' turn toward pornography.

As my reference to jailhouse pornography implies, a great deal of pornography exists unpublished, in the form of manuscript writing or drawing. Even outside the prison context, an enormous number—perhaps even the majority—of pornographic works are in manuscript.[5] The important thing to realize about such manuscripts is that mostly they are produced neither for publication nor for circulation as manuscripts, but for self-enjoyment. Here we have a major difference between prostitution and pornography: hardly any man can, as it were, be his own prostitute (although many try, by attempting auto-fellation),[6] but every man can be his own pornographer. Even a good deal of published pornography was written initially to aid the masturbation of the writer. For example, Jean Genet

[4] Cf. Charles Smith, "Prison Pornography," *Journal of Social Therapy,* Vol. 1 (1955), pp. 126–29, and Stanley B. Zuckerman, "Sex Literature in Prison," *ibid.,* pp. 129–31. I cite these articles merely to document the widespread prison use of pornography.

[5] This seems to be the implication of a statement about quantities made in the Kinsey volume on females, *op. cit.,* p. 672. See also Wladimir Eliasberg, "Remarks on the Psychopathology of Pornography," *Journal of Criminal Psychopathology,* Vol. 3 (1942), pp. 715–20, although on other points, as note 18 below may indicate, Eliasberg is unreliable.

[6] Kinsey *et al.* report in their volume on males, *op. cit.,* p. 510, that "a considerable portion" of males attempt auto-fellation, at least in early adolescence, but that it is anatomically impossible for all except two or three males in a thousand.

indicates that this was why he wrote *Our Lady of the Flowers*.[7] And it is apparently to this motivation that we owe the pornography produced by the most noted pornographer of them all, the Marquis de Sade. Here is a letter from Sade to his wife, written from prison in 1783—a date, note well, that is several years after Sade had begun writing non-pornographic works but before he had written any pornography:

> I'll bet you thought you had a brilliant idea in imposing a revolting abstinence on me with regard to the sins of the flesh. Well, you were all mistaken. You brought my brain to the boiling point. You caused me to conjure up fanciful creatures which I shall have to bring into being.

Over the years that followed, most of them spent in jail, Sade devoted himself to setting down those fanciful creatures on paper. As Albert Camus put it, Sade "created a fiction in order to give himself the illusion of being." [8]

Of course Genet and Sade wrote most of their pornography while in prison. But especially when it comes to sexuality, society imprisons everyone in a number of ways; that is the starting point of Kingsley Davis's argument and mine—and also and originally and profoundly, though Davis is silent on the matter, of Sigmund Freud's. Let us now consider one of those ways—and here my point of departure is Freud rather than Davis—that seems especially germane to our subject.

III

Prostitution and pornography, as we have seen, allow the expression of antisocial sex—impersonal, transitory, nonfamilial sex. But both institutions also provide for antisocial sex in another, deeper sense—one that is merely mentioned in passing by Kingsley Davis but is nevertheless a key function of prostitu-

[7] Cf. Jean Genet, *Our Lady of the Flowers* (New York: Bantam Books, 1964), e.g., pp. 59–61.

[8] I take the Sade and Camus quotations from Georges May, "Fiction Reader, Novel Writer," *Yale French Studies,* No. 35, "Sade" (December, 1965), p. 7.

tion as well as of pornography: these institutions permit "poly-morphous perverse" and other sexual behaviors so highly stig-matized as to be labelled deviant even within the intimacy of marriage and morally inhibited from expression therein.

In other words, sex is socialized by being placed in a double bind—the marital relationship on the one hand and a specified selection of possible sex acts on the other. It is important to see that the function of prostitution and pornography in alleviat-ing the latter constraint is clearly distinct from their providing merely for coitus *per se* (real or imaginary) in an impersonal and transitory relationship.

No real house of prostitution has perhaps approached the logically ultimate one depicted in Genet's play *The Balcony,* where each client buys a custom-made social scene that con-forms in all particulars to any wishful sexual fantasy he chooses to select. But many such houses, as well as freelance prosti-tutes, have specialized in catering to customers who wanted to indulge in sadism, masochism, orgies, intercourse with children, anal or oral intercourse, voyeurism, intercourse with the aid of mechanical contraptions, fetishism, and so on. Among one city's documented examples that come to mind are: London's Victor-ian houses of child prostitutes, including (a sub-specialty of the house) the providing of prepubescent virgins [9]; the adver-tisements by London prostitutes, in their *Ladies Directory* of 1959–1960, offering themselves in rubber or leather clothing; and the many more advertisements, in the same periodical, by prostitutes offering "corrective treatment" and signing them-selves with such sobriquets as "Ex-governess, strict discipli-narian" and "Miss Whyplash." [10] In a study of 732 American clients of prostitutes (574 clients were married, 158 single), the motivation for patronage that the clients indicated most frequently (78 per cent of the clients) was that they "got

[9] Cf. W. T. Stead's series of articles, "Maiden Tribute of Modern Babylon," in issues of the *Pall Mall Gazette* for 1885.

[10] Published monthly in Soho, the *Ladies Directory* was transpar-ently disguised as a directory of "models" in an attempt to circumvent the new ban on open soliciting. At least nine issues appeared. The prosecution of its publisher is described in, e.g., the London *Evening Standard* of July 26, 1960.

something different" from a prostitute, and 10 per cent of these further volunteered the information that the difference was in the type of sexual act performed.[11] Other studies have shown that even the prostitute having no desire to specialize must learn, and quite early in her career, that she will encounter a goodly share of customers presenting "kinky" or "freaky" sexual requests.[12] There is an enormous amount of this sort of material on prostitution (far more than I have mentioned), but, although most of it was available when Davis wrote, he ignores all of it.[13]

[11] Cf. Charles Winick, "Clients' Perceptions of Prostitutes and of Themselves," *International Journal of Social Psychiatry*, Vol. 8 (1961–62), pp. 289–97.

[12] Cf. John Murtagh and Sara Harris, *Cast the First Stone* (New York: McGraw-Hill, 1957), pp. 180–86; James Bryan, "Apprenticeships in Prostitution," *Social Problems*, Vol. 12, No. 3 (Winter, 1965), pp. 287–97.

[13] There are many other defects in Davis's account of prostitution. Most are matters of detail—e.g., Davis thinks the attempt to control pimps arises only with industrialized societies, though Pompeo Molmenti could have told him that in twelfth-century Venice "pimps were imprisoned, branded, tortured, and banished"—but one is crucial: Davis insists that *promiscuity* is the fundamental defining element of prostitution, with commercial and emotionally indifferent aspects of the role being distinctly secondary. But against this emphasis we can put the following considerations: (1) The typical prostitute undertakes intercourse for money or valuables. (2) Even the untypical prostitute, such as one whose prostitution is a religious duty, works for some remuneration, albeit largely for what the economist calls "psychic income." (3) Davis ignores the fact that nymphomaniacs, free souls, and others who literally "give it away" may be stigmatized by the society but are not generally classified as prostitutes either by law enforcers or by laymen (for example, cf. W. F. Whyte, "A Slum Sex Code," *American Journal of Sociology*, Vol. XLIX [July, 1943], pp. 24–31). (4) Davis also ignores the fact that, conversely, some women not promiscuous in the slightest degree, such as concubines, are usually regarded as special types of prostitutes, although they carry lesser stigma. (5) Davis finds support for his "promiscuity" thesis in the fact that the prostitute's stigma is lessened whenever promiscuity is lessened (as in the case of *geisha*, who were selective about customers); but with equal logic one can note that the prostitute's stigma is lessened whenever she is not "strictly commercial," even if she is highly promiscuous (as in the case of temple prostitutes). A definition of prostitution that would best fit all these points—while excluding the woman who "marries for money" as well as the girl who consents to intercourse only after a fancy dinner and is, as Kinsey remarks, "engaged in a more commercialized relationship than she would like to admit"—is the following: Prostitution is the granting of nonmarital sex *as a vocation*.

For our purpose, the point is this: as prostitution goes with respect to perversity, so goes pornography—only more so. Possibly the "more so" derives from the fact that "freaky" sexual interests, being much more highly stigmatized than simple nonmarital coitus, lie closer to total repression or suppression and thus are more often banished strictly to fantasized interaction; possibly other factors account for the difference. In any event, it seems clear that although much pornography depicts sexual relations whose cnly deviance consists of their nonmarital status, an extraordinary amount of this material offers fantasy involvement in sex acts that society proscribes as "unnatural." The history of pornography provides endless examples, and in this regard it makes no difference whether one thinks of the "hard core" tradition from, say, the *Priapea* of ancient Rome to such current paperbacks as *Perverted Lust Slave,* or of the "art" tradition from, say, Petronius to *Histoire d'O.*

IV

From a sociological standpoint, our society's current distinction between "genuine" or "hard core" pornography and highly erotic art is specious in a more fundamental respect.

In recent years the U.S. federal courts have tended to second and extend the view—a view advanced by defense lawyers, literary critics, *et al.*—that certain extremely erotic books and films are not really pornographic because they show over-all serious artistic intent and/or contain other redeeming social virtues, that is, because they seem not to be simply "dirt for dirt's sake." The courts in various ways have reaffirmed and amplified the doctrine, first set forth clearly in Judge John Woolsey's 1933 decision on Joyce's *Ulysses* and the 1934 confirming opinion of Augustus Hand, that highly realistic descriptions of sex cannot be judged pornographic in isolation, but must be viewed within the context of the work as a whole.[14] And except for a handful of diehard clergymen, our social critics, literary scholars, journalists, and the like—our "sociologizers" about pornography—have fallen in line.[15] But the sociologist, at any rate this sociologist, must disagree with such "contextual" arguments and maintain that a work like, say, Henry Miller's *Tropic of Cancer* is pornographic, whatever else it may be in addition.

Granted that in one type of sociological analysis—what is loosely called the "labelling" approach—pornography is neither more nor less than what the society's decisive power groups say it is at any given time, and if our society now chooses officially to label *Tropic of Cancer* non-pornographic, that's that.[16] Such a conceptual framework does lead to many useful discoveries, along the lines indicated by W. I. Thomas's famous dictum that if people define a situation as real, it is real in its consequences. But this mode of analysis has its limitations, as can be seen when we turn to another and equally legitimate mode, functional analysis, and define pornography in terms of what it actually does to or for society—what are its particular uses and effects on people, intended or otherwise.[17]

[14] Judge Woolsey's decision is most readily available in the front matter of the Modern Library edition of *Ulysses*.

[15] Among many recent examples of this kind of reasoning, the best known is probably Eberhard and Phyllis Kronhausen, *Pornography and the Law* (New York: Ballantine Books, 1959).

[16] The "labelling" viewpoint, associated with publications in recent years by Edwin Lemert, Howard Becker, John Kitsuse, *et al.*, is actually a reinvention of a viewpoint formulated and applied in sociology at least as far back as Wilhelm Lange-Eichbaum's *The Problem of Genius* (1931), and in the sociology of deviance at least as far back as Frank Tannenbaum's *Crime and the Community* (1938; see Tannenbaum on "the dramatization of evil"). As a "literary" insight into the workings of society its history goes back much further, e.g., the Spanish inquisitor Salazar Frias wrote in 1611 that "there were neither witches nor bewitched until they were written and talked about." The topic is worthy of a Shandean postscript, but I forbear.

[17] As other parts of this essay should indicate, I am hardly arguing for functionalist theory *against* labelling theory, and rather believe that the two theories apply at different levels of analysis and that both have great explanatory power. But unfortunately some "labellers," in their initial zeal for the reinvented theory, fail to see its limitations. They have overly reified W. I. Thomas's dictum, and are in danger of falling

Pornography obviously has many functions; and some of these are not even sexual—e.g., the providing of paid work for pornography producers and sellers, as well as for their professional opponents. But as we have seen, pornography's main function at the societal level (as distinguished from the individual-psychological level) is to help preserve society's double institutionalization of legitimate sex—within marriage and within a specified few of the possible sex acts—by providing sexual depictions that literally drain off the other, socially illegitimate sexual desires of the beholder. Any sexual depiction (written, recorded, pictorial) that facilitates such masturbatory involvement is thus pornographic. And when pornography is defined in this way, it becomes clear that the courts and the literary critics are wrong, viz., their assumption that pornography and art are mutually exclusive is patently false. For in contemplating naturalistic erotic art, people can and do easily respond to the erotic qualities as such, in utter disregard of the "artistic context." The stock of every pornography store confirms this. Thus the user of written pornography, for example, gets his pornography from "hard core" literature or from erotic "art" literature; so far as he is concerned, the only significant difference is that in the latter he usually gets less for his money. (Hanan Selvin has reminded me that the strong erotic appeal, as such, of much erotic art, is also noted in Sir Kenneth Clark's *The Nude*.)

Let me suggest at this point that my readers think back to their early adolescence and recall the so-called "dirty books"

---

into the same trap W. Lloyd Warner fell into when he concluded that social class is "really" what people say it is.

Thomas's insight is true, but only half the truth. The other half is that social life, though profoundly affected by the participants' linguistic interpretation of it, is not identical with or completely determined by such interpretation. In other words, a real situation has some real consequences even if people *don't* define it as real. That fact is often lost sight of by those who take a "labelling" stance (see, for example, my remarks on Korn and McCorkle in Chapter 3). It is never lost sight of by functionalists; in fact, their recognition of it underlies two of the most useful analytic concepts of modern sociology, the concept of latent function and the concept of functional alternatives.

that were used for adolescent masturbation. (Rather, I ask males among my readers to do this. As the Kinsey data reveal, only a small minority of females are sexually excited by pornography, much less masturbate to it, for reasons largely unknown.[18]) I think most will be able to recall not only "hard core" pornography, such as the little booklets containing pornographic versions of American comic strips, but also that there were so-called "dirty books" which were really for the most part "clean" and were read for their occasional "dirty pages," such as the books of Erskine Caldwell. At least, that was true not only for my own early adolescence but for that of most every other middle-class boy I knew at the time.

I know of no evidence to indicate that people erotically interested in naturalistic descriptions of sex—whatever their age—are seriously impeded by, or even give much thought to, the over-all non-erotic context in which such descriptions might be embedded; and this applies to highly artistic works as well as any other. Can one seriously maintain, for example, that

[18] Note that theories of the female "role" won't do to explain this, for even when men take on all the female role attributes they can, i.e., become hyper-effeminate homosexuals, they do not give up the male's interest in pornography (though of course the object changes and so their pornography consists of erotic depictions of males). And, conversely, when women take on as many male role attributes as they can, i.e., become tough "butch" lesbians, they do not typically lose the female's disinterest in pornography.

There are indeed many pornographic "lesbian" novels, but they are fakes. They are written by men and bought by men. (Both points have been made to me by Times Square pornography peddlers, and I have confirmed the latter from observation in their stores.) The genuine lesbian novel, whether the inartistic kind such as Radclyffe Hall's *Well of Loneliness* or the artistic kind such as Djuna Barnes's *Nightwood,* does not contain naturalistic description of sex but emphasizes the emotional-psychological aspect of sexual relationships. In this respect it is similar to the romantic literature that heterosexual women enjoy (on the latter, see the Kinsey volume on females, *op. cit.,* p. 670).

Apart from disinterest by females (heterosexual or homosexual) in pornography consumption, and the fact that "lesbian" pornography is actually produced by males for males, it has also been established beyond doubt that heterosexual pornography production by females is very rare. (Cf. Kinsey volume on females, *op. cit.,* p. 672.) Yet Wladimir Eliasberg, *op. cit.,* claims a striking feature of pornographic literature is that one cannot tell whether a man or woman is either the producer or consumer.

most of the Americans in Paris who smuggled back copies of
Lady Chatterley's Lover and *Tropic of Cancer* did so out of
interest in the "artistic" or "other social redeeming" qualities
of these books rather than out of "prurient interest"? Or when
it comes to the people—adolescent or adult—who masturbate
to such books, can one seriously claim that they used these
works for masturbatory purposes only so long as our society
labelled them pornographic and stopped such masturbating
when the label changed? Clearly we must modify W. I. Thomas's
dictum, which is the "labelling" dictum writ small, to read that
if people define a situation as real (erotic book X is non-
pornographic), it is real in some of its consequences (erotic
book X can be sold over the counter) but not in others
(people don't stop masturbating to it).

And clearly society has always permitted the dissemination
of some kinds of material that are functionally pornographic.
In our own society one of the major ways it currently does so,
as previously indicated, is to non-label such material as pornographic if it is packaged between significant amounts of non-
erotic material—as in, say, the pages of *Playboy*.

The social processes involved in deciding which pornography shall be permitted, and even some (though by no means
all) of the selective criteria used, are roughly analogous to
the way that—as Sutherland showed us—our society permits
certain types of criminals, notably businessmen who commit
crimes in their corporate capacities, to escape penological consequences and even public stigma.[19] The recent case of *Eros*
notwithstanding, the classier the pornography the more likely
it is to be permitted.[20] What is big news about Ralph Ginzburg

[19] Cf. Edwin Sutherland, *White Collar Crime* (New York: Holt,
Rinehart & Winston, 1949), especially pp. 42 ff. Of course there are
also special selective factors operating at more mundane levels of pornography production. For example, in the recent case of a Michigan
hard-core pornographer who was not only fined $19,000 but sentenced
to ten years in prison, I assume that the severity of the sentence was
not unrelated to the title of his masterpiece: *The Sex Life of a Cop.*
(Cf. New York *Daily News,* April 7, 1966, p. 13, col. 1).

[20] On the case of *Eros* and its publisher, see, for example, *The New
York Times,* March 27, 1966, p. 8E, cols. 1–2.

is precisely what is big news about those price-fixing G.E. officials: such people are rarely the kind who get rapped.

V

At the same time that society permits the dissemination of pornography, it officially denounces it. There is good reason for it to do both at once: from the desire to maintain a restrictive societal definition of "legitimate" sex, it naturally follows that pornography should be stigmatized and harassed yet tolerated as a safety-valve, in the same way that, as Davis demonstrates, society stigmatizes and otherwise harasses prostitution but never really abolishes it.

And just as Davis indicates for prostitution, the stigma attached to pornography is lessened when pornography is tied to some other socially valued end, such as art or science. One important result is this: when the "situation" being defined by society is a naturalistic depiction of sex, the most real consequence of a definition that labels it something other than pornographic is to increase its pornographic use in the society by reducing the inhibitions on acquiring it. This is obvious from the libraries of countless souls who avidly buy highly erotic works that society labels "art" or "literature" or "science" or "scholarship," but who take care not to buy "real" pornography.

And if the non-labeling of an erotic depiction as pornographic actually increases its pornographic use in the society, *de*-labeling increases such usefulness still more. As any publisher can tell you (I speak as a former publisher), it is much better for sales to have an erotic book that was once labeled pornographic and then got de-labeled than to have one that never got labeled at all. Thus such works as *Lady Chatterley* or *Tropic of Cancer* are, functionally, among our society's most pornographic books of all.

All of this could, as Albert Cohen has suggested to me, simply indicate that many if not most Americans label *Playboy* or erotic art or sexual scholarship as "pornography" even if the courts and others don't. But such an interpretation depends on a dubious double hypothesis—that the courts have largely deluded themselves in claiming to follow community opinion and have also failed to mold opinion. It might still be truer than mine, and only empirical data we don't yet have can settle the question. However, I think it more reasonable to suppose this: If the behavior of people often contradicts their attitudes (and social research is forever stumbling against that one), then it can be just as discrepant with their labeling or definition of the situation, and, moreover, such discrepancy is widespread in areas of life involving socially encouraged hypocrisy and unawareness, as in the case of sex behavior.

An even clearer, and more fundamental, discrepancy between social reality and the social definition or labeling of the situation has to do with highly erotic depictions that make no claim to art or science and are not enwrapped in non-erotic contexts, depictions that society calls "hard core pornography" or "dirt for dirt's sake." Such a label means that the material is, in the words of Mr. Justice Brennan, "utterly without redeeming social importance." That definition of the situation is obviously upheld by the great majority of our society; it is entertained equally by the courts, by assorted professional experts (such as literary critics and psychiatrists), and by the lay public. It is, nevertheless, mistaken. To the extent that society, in restricting morally legitimate sex to certain specified acts within marriage, cannot count fully on the mechanisms of repression and suppression, to that extent it must provide stigmatized safety-valve institutions such as prostitution and pornography.[21] As Thomas Aquinas put it—he was explaining

[21] The historical and comparative sociology of the part that "safety-valve" institutions play in social control has yet to be written. We do not even have an adequate general theory of these functions—merely scattered remarks about *panem et circenses*—although Freud has provided many psychological underpinnings for such a theory. Here I note only that in our society major historical changes in safety-valve mechanisms have involved other than sexual institutions; for example, there has been a decrease in displacement of secular goals onto an afterlife (a decline in "pie in the sky" or "opium of the people" functions of religion), and an increase in spectatorship for competitive sports as a means of draining off potential public violence.

prostitution—"A cesspool is necessary to a palace if the whole palace is not to smell." [22]

VI

As I mentioned at the beginning of this chapter, there are many special aspects of the sociology of pornography. One involves a hypothesis I am currently testing and for which I have already found a bit of confirmation, namely, that organized crime is more and more associating itself with the production and distribution of hard core pornography, particularly but not exclusively the most profitable part of it, pornographic movies. This would represent a coming together of organized crime's traditional interest in providing illegal goods and services, with a change in American consumption patterns that is having fateful consequences for the technology of pornography: the great increase, over the past fifteen years, in private ownership of 8 mm. movie projectors.

Until roughly 1950, the pornographic movie business consisted largely in renting films for showing at stag dinners and the like, but since then it has been increasingly, and is now overwhelmingly, a matter of outright sale of prints to individual customers.[23] Consequently, over the past decade and a half, the pornographic movie business has had one of the highest growth rates of any business in the United States (legal or illegal); and organized crime is now well aware of that fact if the general public is not. It is true that the pornographic movie industry, like the pornography industry generally, is still mostly in the hands of individual entrepreneurs; but if present

[22] This view of prostitution—which, shorn of its moralism, is the essence of Davis's sociological view—can be found in many writers beside St. Thomas, e.g., in Horace's *Satires* and Mary Wollstonecraft's *A Vindication of the Rights of Woman*. Of these functionalist explanations prior to Davis, the ablest are in Bernard Mandeville's "An Inquiry into the Origin of Moral Virtue" (his preface to the 1714 edition of *Fable of the Bees*) and his *A Modest Defence of Publick Stews* (1724).

[23] I am informed by pornography distributors in Soho, London, that a similar shift has taken place in England.

trends continue, investment in this industry by organized crime may one day reach the takeoff point, that is, the stage where muscle is applied to make independents fall in line or get out.

There are other special hypotheses about the sociology of pornography that need investigating, dozens of them. What I have tried to do here is offer a general framework within which such investigations might be made.[24]

---

[24] *Addendum:* A detailed scholarly study of mid-Victorian sexuality and pornography, based on the Kinsey collection, was published after this book went to press: Steven Marcus, *The Other Victorians* (New York: Basic Books, 1966). At various places in his book Mr. Marcus discusses the relation of pornography to Victorian society, and his concluding chapter is, in design and in the words of the publisher, "an essay propounding a general theory of pornography as a sociological [i.e., social] phenomenon." In this late note I cannot demonstrate, but only asseverate, that *The Other Victorians* is a prime instance of rubbishy "sociologizing" about pornography, "sociologizing" of the sort produced by that growing band of American literary critics who believe they are experts on society simply because they live in it.

One brief example: Mr. Marcus seems ignorant of statistical reasoning and, worse, of its possible relevance to his argument. Hence one cannot learn from his book that the Victorian era's tremendous upsurge in the growth rate of pornography publishing, which he finds so strange, was equalled and usually surpassed by increases in growth rates for every other kind of publishing. (Indeed, he even seems innocent of the distinction between growth and growth rate.) Nor can one learn that all this had some relation to England's having perfected, in the first decade of the nineteenth century, the Fourdrinier machine for cheap papermaking, nor the fact that, over the following decades, while England's population grew fourfold its *literate* population grew thirty-twofold.

Indexes

Name Index

Subject Index